rich's ride
Hope Changes What's Possible
By Rich Dixon
Foreword by Hal Donaldson

Published by *Simple Plan Media*
Springfield, Missouri 65810

Cover design by Marc McBride — Springfield, Mo.
Cover photo by Gaylon Wampler — Littleton, Colo.

ISBN: 978-0-9886011-0-9

First printing 2012

Printed in the United States of America

rich's ride

Hope Changes What's Possible

By Rich Dixon

Foreword by Hal Donaldson

To Dick Foth —

Thanks for your wisdom, your prayers, and your vision.

Thanks for your incredible ability to connect people.

Thanks for believing in the dream.

contents

FOREWORD....6

INTRODUCTION....8

Part 1: Origins of a Dream....11

1. Blastoff....12
2. Just a Bike Ride....14
3. Hope on Wheels....20
4. *Inceptum Somnii*....24

Part 2: The Journey Begins....37

5. Great Mississippi River Road....38
6. Paul Bunyan's Shadow....42
7. Coincidence, Right?....50
8. Trajectories....58
9. Top of the Hill....64
10. Ride, Rich, Ride....70
11. Peanuts and Shells....76
12. Anschutz Hill....82

13. Fill the Bucket 88

14. Chain of Rocks 92

Photos 102

15. Detours 114

16. Lessons From Cape G 124

17. Dog Evangelism 128

18. Heartsong 134

19. The Middle of Nowhere 140

20. Shotgun House 146

21. Rolling Fork 150

22. I Can Do This 158

23. Canine Philosophy 164

Part 3: Aftermath 173

24. Success! 174

25. Next? 182

ACKNOWLEDGMENTS 190

foreword

Hope Changes What's Possible

In 2012, Rich Dixon embarked on an adventure down the Mississippi River that would raise tens of thousands of dollars for Convoy of Hope, inspire countless people, and show the world that hope truly changes what's possible.

Each year, Convoy of Hope helps millions of people who are suffering. We have more than 126,000 children enrolled in our children's feeding initiatives throughout the world. We also respond to disasters such as the earthquake in Haiti. We also conduct dozens of outreaches each year where "honored guests" receive free health screenings, family portraits, clothing, shoes, school supplies, and groceries.

One thing is for certain: Convoy of Hope could not bring help to hurting people without real-life heroes like Rich — people who put others first and oftentimes serve in the background with little recognition or fanfare. Such people also sacrifice time and finances so that the poor and suffering can have a shot at a better life.

I'm so thankful Convoy of Hope became friends with Rich. By handcycling down the Mississippi River, he raised money to feed children in our programs in seven countries throughout the world, and inspired countless people to make a difference in the world.

In 2012, Rich received our "Volunteer of the Year" award. It was a fitting prize for an individual who did so much to help Convoy of Hope make the world a better place.

As you read this book, my hope is that Rich's story will inspire you to do great things. The kinds of things that are beyond you ... The kinds of things that can change the world ... The kinds of things that tell the world that with hope anything is possible. ▮

Hal Donaldson
President, Convoy of Hope

introduction

A dream is a story waiting to be written.

On September 12, 2011, I began an eight-week bike ride. I cranked the entire length of the Mississippi River from Lake Itasca, Minnesota, to New Orleans. In cycling terms, my nine-miles-per-hour average speed was pretty slow, so maybe I should reveal one additional bit of information: I was riding a handcycle. I'm a wheelchair user, and I pedaled the entire fifteen hundred miles with my arms.

This ride was a longstanding dream. And, as I mentioned, a dream is a story waiting to be written.

A dream offers an opportunity to travel an unexplored path toward the remarkable and follow a vision that's audacious and scary and completely outrageous. A dream invites you to follow your passions and gifts, to write an amazing story of service to others. You're the author; the pages are the hours and days of your life. The words are the choices with which you fill those pages.

You write an amazing story by choosing to follow the dream.

Dream-followers change the world. They change the world because they choose to invest in possibilities and explore limits rather than settle for status quo safety. They choose courage over cowardice, risk over security, and the prospect of falling over the certainty of motionlessness.

Impossible dream is an oxymoron. Many accomplishments once seemed impossible ... until someone did them. Dreamers tackle what's impossible until it becomes merely improbable; then they continue until it becomes inevitable.

We're all dreamers. Our culture tells us dreams are impractical and dreamers are irresponsible, so dreams often remain dormant. But the dream remains, waiting for the dreamer to follow and write its story.

I finally decided to follow my dream. This book is the story of what happened.

I invite you to join us for this bike ride that became something else. Along the way you'll meet amazing people and hear inspiring stories of courage and perseverance. You'll perceive the Mississippi River from a new perspective, and experience its nuances and subtleties as it grows and changes along with the dream it represents. I'll share some insights, observations, and lessons learned. I hope you'll discover something useful and find a deeper connection with God.

Perhaps, somewhere along the way, you'll encounter your own dream and unearth some lurking desire you thought you'd buried. If we're lucky, our journey along the Mississippi River might become the story of what happens when you discover and follow your dream. ▮

part 1

origins of a dream

1 blastoff

You are one idea away from a totally different life.

The hard-packed dirt clearing provided an ideal venue for the opening scene of an improbable script. Secluded beneath a lush forest canopy and surrounded on three sides by a dense wall of Minnesota forest, four people and a curious dog assembled around a bright yellow handcycle at the north end of Lake Itasca. Cool breezes whispered through the trees; early morning sunlight reflected a stunning blue sky across the lake's glassy surface. A hundred miles from the Canadian border in early September, this was about as good as it gets.

Behind us, water splashed over a man-made rock wall into the tourist-friendly pool marking the official headwaters of the Mississippi River. My dog, Monte, sniffed curiously at every stray smell. Parked at the water's edge, the low, sleek handcycle seemed to struggle against invisible restraints as it waited impatiently for the preliminaries to end. The bike and I faced a shared journey along the great river's course. After more than ten years of imagining and months of training and preparation, we were anxious to begin.

Clicking cameras documented the occasion. My cousin Mark and our friend Steve dipped the bike's back tires in the pool. Steve's prayer sought God's blessing and guidance. We glanced at each other, surveyed the idyllic scene, and hesitated like actors awaiting the director's next command. We needed someone to yell, "Action!"

Our impromptu commencement ceremony lacked musical overture, cheering crowds, or any official suggestion of grand significance. The momentous episode demanded creative camera angles and a hidden orchestra's crescendo, but eagerly expected epic events often plop into real life with a disappointing sense of anticlimax. So Mark, Steve, and my wife, Becky, watched as I climbed slowly onto the bike from my wheelchair. Helmet, gloves, feet adjusted, Monte's leash attached to the bike's frame—

I took one last look around a scene I didn't want to forget.

"Time to go."

I pushed on the cranks, and the bike moved slowly across the clearing while Becky scrambled to shoot some video of my less-than-illustrious exit. With Monte trotting alongside, I followed the path up a small hill and disappeared into the trees toward the visitor center.

As I cranked through the woods—alone now with excitement and uncertainty—I understood the common course shared by the dream, the river, and me. Tiny beginnings of the mighty river bubbled beside the narrow path where gravel crunched beneath my tires. Shoulder muscles complained about sudden exertion. Cool morning air washed across my face as I surveyed the tranquil beauty.

Dreams choose you. God planted this dream in my heart. Finally, I said yes.

The journey was underway, but this wasn't the beginning.

You are one idea away from a totally different life.

2 just a bike ride

The long road to "amazing" usually begins at "crazy."

I really just wanted to go for a bike ride, initially.

I didn't intend to create an elaborate project, a cool website, or another blog. I didn't consider branding, logos, taglines, or media exposure, didn't think about fund-raising partnerships or sponsors. I didn't begin with a clear vision, a mission statement, or measurable goals. I didn't want a small circle of key advisors or an enormous circle of supporters. This entire project began with a simple desire to do an extended bike ride.

It was a crazy idea that changed everything. I really was one idea away from a totally different life.

I started handcycling in 1999, twelve years after a senseless accident caused a spinal cord injury and confined me to a wheelchair with paralysis below my chest. I cycled thousands of miles around my hometown of Fort Collins, Colorado. I'm blessed to live in a cycling-friendly community at the base of the Rocky Mountain foothills. For more than a decade, as I cranked familiar streets and trails near my home, I secretly harbored the dream of doing some sort of cross-country ride. Honestly, I didn't believe a guy in a wheelchair could accomplish such an outrageous goal.

In story lingo, three inciting incidents challenged my faith in impossibility. One was a movie titled *The Bucket List*, a story about two old guys who survive cancer and realize they don't have forever to live their dreams. The second was my sixtieth birthday in 2011, a tangible reminder of my own limited time frame. The third was a book—Donald Miller's *A Million Miles in a Thousand Years*. Don wrote about looking at life as a story and challenged readers to write better, more interesting stories with their own lives.

Every good story involves a character who wants something and overcomes conflict to get it. I was the character. This crazy bike ride, this item on my bucket list, was what I wanted. I needed to overcome the obstacles posed by my disability, as well as my own self-imposed limitations, if I wanted to write a more interesting story with the remaining years of my life.

The long road to "amazing" usually begins at "crazy." By any measure, a cross-country bike ride by a guy in a wheelchair is a bizarre notion. It's risky and expensive and impractical. It would have been a lot easier to just forget the whole thing, but finally I knew I wanted a worthwhile story more than I wanted safety and security.

I began talking seriously about this nutty idea in December of 2010. Once Becky realized I wasn't going to let it go, she sought guidance from our friend, Pastor Dick Foth. His visionary mind immediately saw opportunities far beyond what I allowed myself to imagine. Dick helped us recruit a dozen local companies who sponsored the entire cost of the trip, and we began to sketch outlines for Rich's Ride: Together on a Journey of Hope.

Timberline Church in Fort Collins has been our home for more than a decade. We're blessed by a large church family with gifted leaders and an amazing sense that following Jesus happens beyond the walls of a building. We're constantly challenged and encouraged, and people were eager to support and participate in this audacious, God-sized dream. As ridiculous as it seemed, my simple bike ride became a full-fledged church-adopted missions outreach project. Missions expert Pastor Mark Orphan added the final bit of insanity when he declared, "You realize you're now a missionary."

Who ... me? I can't be a missionary! Missionaries attend Bible colleges and receive some clear, mysterious message straight from God about their anointed purpose in life. Missionaries drop everything and go to dangerous places and perform miracles. Missionaries are special. I'm just a messed-up guy who wanted to take a bike ride. I'd rather write a check and hire special folks with some specific calling. Let them be responsible for ministry.

Except, of course, that's not the way Jesus did it. He picked ordinary, uneducated people, outcasts, social misfits, the worst of the worst. He hung out with them, equipped them, and sent them to accomplish the most important tasks in history. He chose regular people because not much ministry will get accomplished if we wait for the perfect folks to do it.

I'll let you in on a secret, just between us. Dick really heard and encouraged me to embrace what I was afraid to say out loud. I wanted to share the dream, but I was afraid to believe God could help an ordinary guy do something extraordinary. I was afraid to act like I believed what Jesus said was true.

Fear makes it easier to wish you could than to hope you can.

Hope isn't a wish. It's a confident expectation based on faith in God's promises. Wishing traps you on the sidelines and keeps you focusing on the reasons you probably can't play. Hope gets you into the game. I needed Becky and Dick Foth and the other folks who joined this outrageous dream to help me stop wishing and discover within myself a story of hope I could share with others.

A new friend, Dick DeCook, became a trusted advisor and an amazing prayer supporter with an incredible heart for missions. Through many late-winter meetings we hatched the outline for Rich's Ride. I'd crank my handcycle fifteen hundred miles along the length of the Mississippi River, beginning at Lake Itasca in northern Minnesota and concluding eight weeks later in New Orleans. Becky would drive, tow a trailer, and serve as chief organizer and one-person pit crew. Monte, my Labrador retriever service dog, would run a few miles each day and provide comic relief.

Along the route we'd talk about our story, about hope, dreams, and possibility, and about Jesus. We'd share our experience, believing God would use the conversations to inspire others to confront adversity with courage and confidence.

And we'd raise funds for our new partner, Convoy of Hope. We'd talk about their humanitarian mission to advance justice by providing food, clean water, and disaster relief to those in need.

The project nearly died in infancy. In March, just as we began to put plans in place, I landed in the hospital. An infection in an especially tender spot where backside meets wheelchair kept me off the bike for ten weeks. Docs finally cleared me to resume training in mid-June, and we were go for blastoff from Lake Itasca on September 12, 2011.

Preparing for the trip of a lifetime during an incredibly hectic summer, I was almost too busy to be scared. In private moments, alone on training rides, I frequently wondered what in the world I'd gotten myself into, but it was too late to back out. Too many people were involved. I was either going to do this crazy ride or collapse somewhere beside the river.

It was a God-inspired desire to do something bigger than I could possibly accomplish on my own. Becky and I knew we were stepping into the unknown, and we prepared with an odd mixture of my anxiety and her calm assurance. We knew we couldn't do this by ourselves, and we were trusting God for guidance and provision. It wasn't because we felt comfortable. We simply had no other choice.

God had us right where He wanted us.

As we prepared, I recalled a Scripture passage from the conclusion of my previous book, *Relentless Grace*. This promise of God was a central element of our wedding, and now it seemed meaningful and appropriate in this new context. You'll see frequent references to this passage along the journey, because I kept it in front of me as I thought and wrote and prayed.

Forget the former things;
do not dwell on the past.
See, I am doing a new thing!
Now it springs up; do you not perceive it?
I am making a way in the wilderness
and streams in the wasteland. (Isaiah 43:18–19)

I believe God wanted me to perceive the new thing He was doing through us, and to encourage others to look for the new thing He's doing in their lives. Perhaps as we take this bike ride together, you'll perceive the new thing He's doing in your life.

Our church family offered incredible support as we prepared and trained. The Sunday before we left town, Pastor Dick Foth wanted to send us off with a blessing. So in front of our large congregation he introduced the project and said, "Rich, why don't you tell us a bit of what this is all about."

"Well, I really just wanted to go for a bike ride ..."

The long road to "amazing" usually begins at "crazy."

notes

3 hope on wheels

People respond to hope.

The trailer and its sign turned out to be a choice of pure genius.

Timberline Church loaned us a small enclosed utility trailer to haul the handcycle along with equipment and supplies for eight weeks on the road. The trailer's sides displayed our sponsors' names below the RICH'S RIDE logo and our tagline: Together on a Journey of Hope.

Like most successful aspects of the project, the sign and its design were Becky's ideas. I don't think either of us had any notion of how many conversations would begin because of attention grabbed by our rolling billboard. Becky would pull into a gas station, hotel, or store, someone would ask what the trailer was about, and she'd launch into her story. Becky loves telling the story of God's hope. She was the true spokesperson for this project. I just rode a bike.

It happened dozens of times, but my favorite example occurred outside New Orleans in a small hospital lobby. While Becky waited for me to use the accessible restroom, a group approached and asked her to tell them about "Hope on Wheels," their summary of the sign's message. The trailer once again opened the door to a conversation about hope.

"Hope" was always in the DNA of Rich's Ride. We knew the theme would center on biblical hope, a confident expectation based on faith. Hope allows you to believe, despite the evidence, and then watch the evidence change. Hope lets you sit at the bottom of a hill you know you can't climb—and then crank to the top.

The "official" tagline for Rich's Ride developed in a roundabout way. In December of 2010 I started telling Becky I was serious about doing this ride. As my kind, supportive wife, she would smile and nod, secretly hoping (I'm sure) I'd forget the whole crazy idea. This cycle repeated several times before we started talking seriously about how we might approach something so outrageous.

A few weeks into 2011 our pastor delivered one of those beginning-of-the-year sermons, including a new church theme: "Together on the Journey." Maybe God was passing along a message. When we got around to developing a tagline, we settled on "Together on a Journey of Hope."

The tagline captured what we envisioned—a community centered on walking together in hope. I believe we're all together on this journey. But when we designed the bike jerseys, I knew the phrase we'd feature on the back. It was my personal mantra for the ride and the improbable process behind it. Above the cross of Christ the jersey proclaimed:

HOPE changes what's possible.

Convoy of Hope

The folks at Convoy of Hope address some of the most desperate, basic, daily needs of those on the edge of survival. I felt really comfortable about our partnership, but I don't particularly like fund-raising. Asking people for money, even for a worthy cause, feels awkward. The prospect of finding sponsors and using Rich's Ride as a fund-raiser made me uncomfortable.

On the other hand, I recognized a potentially significant opportunity. We knew our story would touch folks, and the impact would be multiplied through the blog (www.richsride.org/blog) and social media. If we could leverage our efforts to raise funds and awareness for a worthy effort, it seemed kind of selfish not to do so.

But how do you select a "worthy" cause? Across this country and around the world, incredibly selfless people dedicate talent and energy to address poverty, slavery, abuse, hunger, disease, clean water, violence, homelessness, education ... the list seems endless.

My search for the "right" cause or organization taught me a couple of things.

First, there's no single correct answer. You pray and listen to your heart and talk to people you trust. It's important to investigate, but in the end you trust God to lead you in the right direction.

Second, selecting one doesn't mean rejecting the others. They're all important, but trying to do everything really means doing nothing. Choosing is tough when everyone markets their cause with pictures of starving, abused children; filthy water; and wounded veterans. This world is broken, and it's not my job to fix it. God's taking care of that, in His timing. I'm called to make a difference by simply doing what I can, where I am, with what I have.

Seeking the "right" mission can create a sense of guilt that's one of the enemy's most powerful tools. Guilt splinters efforts and renders them ineffective. It steals the joy of serving. It can immobilize and prevent us from doing anything.

God isn't about guilt. He wants wise, prayerful selections; but mostly He wants us to serve with passion, freedom, and joy. So we choose as wisely as possible and trust Him to bless our efforts.

Once we made a decision, our partnership with Convoy of Hope just felt right. They provided significant disaster relief following devastating 2011 tornadoes. Our route passed directly through some of the affected areas, so we knew people would be sympathetic. Convoy of Hope also serves hungry people, especially children, across the U.S. and around the world.

But representing Convoy of Hope along the ride was curious, because we rarely talked at length about the organization itself. Becky and I talked a lot about Jesus and hope and our story of overcoming adversity, and we'd almost casually mention our fund-raising efforts for this organization. Sometimes folks would ask and we'd provide more details, but usually they were less interested in the organization than the mission.

I didn't think much about this unusual dynamic until the ride ended and we had the opportunity to visit the Convoy of Hope headquarters in Springfield, Missouri. We toured their incredible facility, including a warehouse the size of six football fields filled with donated disaster-relief supplies. I was invited to speak to the staff at their chapel service the following morning.

As I looked at this group of dedicated people, I understood why we didn't need to talk about Convoy of Hope. "You folks aren't here to serve an organization, are you?" Heads shook.

They were there to serve people and make a difference in the world. Their organization was a tool, but it wasn't what touched people's hearts. It made perfect sense to talk about hope without "promoting" an organization. Our connection was organic and natural. When we told our story of hope we were already telling their story as well.

As I said, I don't like fund-raising. I don't recall a single time when we specifically asked people for money, but they gave generously anyway. Rich's Ride raised nearly $60,000 to feed hungry children. Through Convoy of Hope's incredibly efficient feeding initiatives, those dollars will feed twelve hundred kids for an entire year. It doesn't solve world hunger or fix the world. It does change the world for twelve hundred kids.

People respond to hope.

4 inceptum somnii

Don't allow your resources to determine your vision.

You don't choose your dreams. Dreams choose you.

You don't dictate a dream's nature or its path. A dream is its own thing, prompted by God, born in the indiscernible depths of your soul at the intersection of passions, gifts, and service. You don't pursue a dream as though you can catch it, tie it down, and be done with it. A dream invites and inspires and offers to lead on an adventure. You choose only whether to follow or turn away.

I tried to rebuff this dream. For more than ten years I was absolutely certain it was the product of ridiculous self-delusion. I substituted lesser adaptations, tried to modify its course, and pretended I could satisfy its call on some more convenient path. I desperately sought some more reasonable alternative.

But this God-sized dream eventually demanded a decision. I could either turn away from the dream or seek God's help as I stared directly into its face. And finally I had to acknowledge that a God big enough to inspire this impossibly big dream was also big enough to provide a way to follow it.

A God-sized dream is a frightening thing. This one exceeded my ability and stretched far beyond my vision. Even the most optimistic analysis led to one obvious conclusion: I lacked the necessary resources, skills, physical capability, and support system. Mother Teresa once said, "I know God won't give me more than I can handle." Then she added, "I just wish He didn't trust me so much."

A God-sized dream isn't about what I can do. I questioned God's judgment, certain He had overestimated my ability or perhaps gotten me mixed up with someone else. But God-sized dreams are impossible, without God. Perhaps that's the whole point.

See, I am doing a new thing!
Now it springs up; do you not perceive it?

Where does a dream begin?

Sometimes we describe God-ordained projects or journeys as though they commenced in some obvious, unmistakable, inevitable manner. We imagine God leaving a pile of stones to officially and precisely mark the starting point, but I don't seem to receive such obvious cosmic directions. The dream actually seems to originate and progress much like the river.

Explorer Henry Schoolcraft generally gets credit for "discovering" Lake Itasca as the Mississippi River's source. He even changed the lake's Native American name (*Omashkoozo-zaaga'igan* or Elk Lake) by combining letters from the Latin words *veritas* (truth) and *caput* (head). A Latin name apparently imparted some sense of official certainty, but locating the "true head" wasn't quite as simple as it sounds. Schoolcraft's expedition backtracked along the river's course through a maze of lakes and ponds connected by small streams, eventually declaring the north end of this particular lake as the origin of the mighty Mississippi River.

However, Lake Itasca itself is fed by smaller streams formed from trickles produced by raindrops. So I suppose it's a question of how far back you wish to go. At some point the explorers apparently chose a logical spot.

It's interesting to look at the source of the river and realize it isn't a river ... until it is. One moment it's a swampy bog at the end of a lake, and then it's a river. The exact moment of transition isn't clearly defined.

Of course we can go back—after the fact—and erect a sign with a Latin inscription lending credibility to a less-than-certain declaration. At the Mississippi headwaters a neat rock wall clearly delineates where lake ends and river begins. You can stand at the exact spot where the river's path begins. It's a great place to take cheesy tourist photos, but it's all artificial. The wall's man-made.

rich's ride *By Rich Dixon*

The river's true beginning is messy and uncertain. You can't really know it's a river ... until it is. The precise starting point matters less than recognizing that the river's path takes you in a direction worth following.

It's the same with dreams.

Dreams aren't manufactured through some well-defined, predetermined process. You don't wake up one day and decide to conjure a God-sized dream. A real dream is born in the dreamer's head and heart and spirit, present long before it's acknowledged. By the time you know it's there, the dream has already assumed an identity.

Much like the river, a dream is recognized somewhere downstream. The only way to locate the source is to backtrack and decide how far to go. To identify the beginning of the dream, you check each decision point until you discover the logical place to begin the narrative.

Like the river, the precise beginning of a dream isn't important if the dream's path takes you in a direction worth following. What really matters is what you do with the dream once you recognize its presence. But there's some fascination in retracing the course to see where it originated. Perhaps something about the particular point of departure might help me understand the foundation beneath my dream, allow me to project forward, and help me follow the dream's truth.

Since my injury signifies the beginning of a second life, I'm tempted to wander back to December 5, 1987. The fall and the chaotic hours in a trauma center dramatically altered my course. But I think the injury and the wheelchair and the tale of *Relentless Grace* form the backstory. Paralysis, depression, God's faithfulness, a circle of friends who wouldn't let me quit on life—these and many other streams fed into a specific event at the true genesis of this improbable journey.

So I'll go back to a cloudy gray day in the spring of 1999 and erect a sign. Following Schoolcraft's example, I'll letter my marker in Latin to add an artificial sense of inevitability. Let's snap some mental photos in front of an official-looking proclamation: *Inceptum Somnii*—The Beginning of the Dream.

Handcycle 1.0

Excitement, apprehension, embarrassment—I wasn't sure what I felt as I stared at the shiny new contraption. Sitting with three guys in the quiet neighborhood street in front of my Fort Collins home, I could only wonder why I consented to this craziness. Well-meaning therapists and friends tried for years after the injury to engage me in alternative forms of recreation. Adaptive skiing, wheelchair basketball, and quad rugby sparked no interest. I was too busy being angry and afraid to acknowledge the obvious need, and my secret internal desire, for some kind of physical outlet.

I'm still not sure what made handcycling different. Maybe my encouragers simply wore me down until I got tired of saying no. In retrospect it seems like a precious instant, an answer to hundreds of prayers. I sincerely believe God used the handcycle to finally guide me out of darkness and despair, but that perception crystallized much farther downstream.

At the time, I didn't recognize a watershed moment and the birth of a life-altering passion. I didn't identify this seemingly nondescript day as *Inceptum Somnii*. I perceived only my brand-new twenty-five-hundred-dollar toy and my intense fear.

Secretly I was eager to get going. Ten years after my injury I was finally sick of mostly sitting inside and the sham of pretending to exercise while really doing almost nothing. I'd grown tired of my own complaining and lack of effort. I desperately wanted to believe I could accept the challenge of doing something physical again.

But well-rehearsed habits don't just disappear. A decade of giving up told me this wasn't going to work out. When you say "I can't" enough times, it becomes your default belief. I quit trying because I was convinced I couldn't succeed because I wouldn't try. I trapped myself in a difficult-to-reverse death spiral. As badly as I wanted to learn to ride the strange machine, my brain told me I'd fail. My heart told me I didn't need another disappointment. My spirit told me nothing could bring meaning to a damaged, broken life. Every inner voice screamed hopeless!

I'd like to report an act of heroic trust. I wish I could claim I resolutely pushed through the resistance, rebuked those demonic internal pressures, and boldly stepped forward in faith. A conscious, courageous decision would certainly create a more compelling scene in the made-for-TV movie.

Reality paints a less gallant picture. I effectively backed myself into a corner from which there was no easy escape. I had already spent a bunch of money on a handcycle I wasn't even sure I could ride. My buddies delivered the new bike and stood around waiting to help me get started. I had to give it a try.

Maybe "stepping out in faith" isn't always a valiant act of superhuman courage and absolute certainty. Maybe acting on faith means making big commitments and then wondering, *What in the world have I gotten myself into?* Maybe it's moving forward when every shred of logic says you're crazy. Maybe God really wants you to commit beyond your own ability.

What if "stepping out in faith" really means making commitments that back you into a corner with no side door and intentionally putting yourself in a situation in which your only option is trust? What if it means dreaming big, thinking you can do it on your own, and then leaning on God's promises when you realize the dream requires something far beyond your own ability?

Sometimes tales of great faith are portrayed through a revisionist lens, as though a successful outcome was inevitable. You're supposed to believe if you pray hard enough and trust God enough you can't fail. But where there's no uncertainty, there's no need for faith. If the outcome's assured, why bother with trust? I wonder if more folks would trust God and step forward in faith if they knew it usually means facing fear and doubt and moving ahead anyway when you're certain only of God's faithfulness.

I moved forward because it was the only way out of the corner. I pasted a false sense of assurance on my face, rolled up to the bike in the middle of the street, and tentatively lifted one lifeless leg over the frame. With a lot of help I managed to lower myself onto the seat and into an unfamiliar new position. I felt uncomfortable and unstable, but it was too late to turn back. After so many years spent clinging to my misguided notion of false security, I'd moved out of my comfort zone. Looking back, I see God had me right where He wanted me.

My friends adjusted the footrests and helped with proper positioning. My inner cynic knew I'd never be able to ride without a full-time pit crew. While I mentally listed all the tasks I couldn't perform, my buddies completed the adjustments. No more excuses. It was time to begin.

I placed my hands on the cranks and pushed.

I'm not sure what I expected. I didn't imagine an instant transformation from sedentary whiner to handcycle all-star. I knew all those years of inactivity took a toll on strength and endurance. I knew it wouldn't be easy, but I was entirely unprepared for the result of my initial shove on the hand grips.

Nothing.

Absolutely nothing. I braced against the backrest, strained with all the power in my stick-arms, and the stupid bike didn't budge. In ideal conditions on a smooth, level street, I couldn't move the bike a single inch.

At first I thought I was the victim of a prank. Obviously my buddies somehow sabotaged the bike, or maybe one of them was standing behind me grabbing the wheels. But nobody was laughing. Then I remembered the shifters. Maybe I needed to start in an easier gear. No such luck—I was already using the easiest of twenty-one possibilities.

So there I sat with absolutely no obstacles or excuses, and I couldn't budge. I recall feeling overwhelmed and utterly discouraged. I finally took a risk, tried something new, allowed myself to get excited about the possibility of experiencing enjoyment, and I couldn't even begin.

Not exactly the anticipated mystical moment of *Inceptum Somnii*.

My volunteer pit crew checked the machine, verified the gears and adjustments, and reported I should be "go" for liftoff. No apparent mechanical issues prevented me from blasting into the new frontier. Clearly the problem was the bike's inadequate propulsion system.

I've learned to enjoy cycling precisely because the passenger is also the engine. Beyond a certain point, better equipment can't take you faster or farther. Better riding requires a better "me." This bike's engine needed a lot of work!

As simplistic as it sounds, sometimes the only way to begin is to get moving. One of my friends gave me a shove and I rolled off on my initial handcycle adventure. I coasted along, testing steering and brakes, and noticed for the first time the slight slope of my familiar street. This allowed me to crank a few times and regain a bit of shattered confidence. I felt the breeze on my face and allowed myself to savor an unfamiliar sense of independent motion. Handcycling was really cool!

I reached the end of the block, managed to turn around, and faced a harsh cycling reality: downhill in one direction means uphill in the other. The nearly imperceptible decline now confronted me as a suburban Kilimanjaro. Old habit reminded me I'd surely fail. If I couldn't crank downhill without help, how could I possibly get back to my friends at the top of the mountain?

What's the point of even attempting the impossible? I should have just quit and waited for my buddies walking toward me, but instead I discovered a principle to sustain and encourage me in dozens of "impossible" situations. This principle became a foundation beneath the dream:

Hope changes what's possible.

Most of us underestimate our capabilities. We settle for less because we mistakenly invest in our own inability. We don't even approach our capacity because we believe in our weakness instead of God's strength. As my friends walked down the street to save me, I placed my hands on the cranks once again. I braced, pushed, and a miracle occurred.

I rolled forward!

My halting movement certainly didn't threaten any world records, unless there's a mark for slowest ride ever. It wasn't smooth and it wasn't pretty. But my rescuers applauded as I cranked past them and back to my starting point.

Maybe you think I'm exaggerating by classifying my painfully slow journey up an insignificant incline as a miracle. Just a few moments earlier I absolutely could not move the bike. I strained and pushed as hard as I could and couldn't roll a single inch. Cranking the bike was literally impossible, but now I rolled past cheering supporters. When something's impossible and then it occurs, you find yourself in the presence of the miraculous.

Did a one-block ride make me magically stronger? Of course not. Sitting at the bottom of an imperceptible rise, I was still the weak, out-of-shape, stick-armed guy who tried and failed to move the bike. God didn't infuse my skinny shoulders with some sort of spiritual power.

I wasn't stronger, but something had changed. My simple excursion along one unremarkable neighborhood street inspired faith. I actually believed I could do it, and belief changed everything. Hope—an expectation based on faith. God helped me discover hope and allowed me to breach an impenetrable barrier. What seemed physically impossible became merely difficult.

By any definition, that's a miracle.

Hope changes what's possible.

One-Degree Miracles

My first handcycle ride wasn't quite the epic adventure I'd imagined. After one trip down the block and back, I felt exhausted. My shoulders ached, and I could barely raise my arms. I needed a lot of help to lift off the seat and into my chair. I still harbored a good deal of doubt. Would I be able to transfer on and off the bike, get my feet positioned, and ride without assistance? Would I get beyond my two-block limit? Would I ever ride well enough to actually have fun?

We discourage other dreamers when we pretend our dreams began with trumpets and a hand-delivered invitation from a burning bush. We play make-believe, as though the dream appeared in full form with clear direction and unmistakable mandate.

rich's ride *By Rich Dixon*

Dreams begin like rivers. You have to follow the dream, live with it for a while, before you even perceive it. Just like the river, the dream becomes obvious somewhere downstream.

So why bother backtracking, searching for an indefinable origin? Why bother expending the effort to find an elusive source? Once the dream's developed, does it even matter where it began?

I think it does, because we learn from experience. We learn when we retrace our steps. When you look at where you are, often it's difficult to determine any sense of direction. Looking back allows you to see patterns and better understand how you reached a particular position. And sometimes, when you project forward from those experiences, you get a clearer idea about your future trajectory.

Life mostly doesn't consist of huge changes and momentous decisions. Your present situation is the accumulated result of thousands of small choices over months and years. We want to believe we can change course in an instant, but altering your long-term path is more like steering an aircraft carrier. Rather than instantaneous ninety-degree turns, life is more about one-degree corrections.

We don't like slow, small change. We want to see results right now, and one-degree turns take a long time to show up. A one-degree course change on a ten-foot journey only alters your final position by about two inches, but if you maintain the same one-degree alteration for one thousand miles your location changes by more than seventeen miles.

Each of us is one small choice, a single one-degree course correction, from a radically altered life that won't usually show up immediately. Life is long-term because God is long-term. Certainly there are times when God steps in and causes an instant one-eighty. But more often He works through everyday situations and circumstances.

I moved a bike I couldn't move; a miracle changed my course, but an observer wouldn't have recognized it. The miracle's only apparent downstream after thousands of miles when you realize you're a long distance from where the original course would have led. It's a one-degree miracle, and it alters everything.

It's not water to wine, but it's no less a miracle.

Goal #1

A new habit emerged. Nearly every day I'd slide myself awkwardly onto the bike and struggle to lift my feet onto the footrests. I'd coast down the driveway and crank slowly around the block. Gradually my rides became a block or two longer, imperceptible progress always clouded by skepticism and doubt. I was sure I'd never do much more than struggle around my own neighborhood.

The one-degree miracle wasn't creating instant magic, but I was on a radically different path even if I didn't yet perceive it. One day, as May melted into June, I encountered an initial signal of significant change. I consciously decided on a goal.

I knew just riding aimlessly wouldn't keep me motivated. I knew I'd quit as soon as the process became difficult or repetitive. If I truly wanted to make progress, I needed a big target. So one day I told some friends I planned to ride a thousand miles during the summer.

It was an insane notion. As I completed my twenty-fifth year of teaching math in a public school classroom, about eighty days separated the last and first days of school in 1999. At a time when I could scarcely ride a block or two without stopping and a maximum workout covered less than two miles, I committed to an average daily ride of 12.5 miles. Everyone believed I had overreached and set myself up for failure. Concerned friends suggested a more reasonable objective. No one, including myself, actually believed I would succeed.

I sincerely believe a thousand miles was God's answer to innumerable prayers for a sense of purpose. He'd been preparing me for a challenge, and He knew this was the proper time. Others tried for years to penetrate my walls of despair and resistance, but His timing isn't ours. He's patient, and when the correct moment arrived He placed me in just the right circumstances and stirred an "impossible" trial to motivate and inspire me.

He didn't make it easy. God usually doesn't place His answers in our hands. Instead, He places them within our reach and offers to journey with us as we move toward them.

Without actually believing I'd succeed, friends supported me. They appeared at sunrise to ride along, inquired about my progress, and encouraged me. My circle of supporters intentionally lifted me up and pushed me forward on the most difficult physical quest I'd ever undertaken.

To be honest, "difficult" doesn't come close to capturing the hard work. After so many idle years, I dragged myself out of bed each morning. Aching and sore, I gulped breakfast and struggled onto the bike. I could manage average speeds of five or six miles per hour on good days, and many days weren't good. My rides seemed ponderously slow, and I doubt if I ever cranked more than a couple of miles without stopping.

Most days I did two rides, morning and evening, to log the necessary miles. As days faded in summer heat, I passed a hundred, then five hundred miles. Rides became progressively longer, though not much faster. The mileage chart on my computer spreadsheet climbed. And then it happened.

On an ordinary August evening, the day before school started, my odometer read 1000.0.

My thousand-mile summer marked a turning point. Please don't paint some romantic mental picture of roses and sunshine, because it's hurtful to revise history to create a mythical instant turnaround. Invented epiphanies can actually discourage others. It wasn't easy, and it wasn't magic. It was mostly hard work; sweat; and slow, painstaking, one-crank-at-a-time progress.

The turning point arrived because I perceived a tangible result from a one-degree miracle. I finally stuck with a commitment long enough to notice a substantially better result from a small change in direction. However, 1000.0 didn't conclude a story because it wasn't really a destination. It concluded a chapter and placed a marker along a much longer journey.

Where does a dream begin?

See, I am doing a new thing!
Now it springs up; do you not perceive it?

God says clearly He's doing a "new thing" in my life, but He implies it's right in front of me yet still difficult to see. I need to open my eyes and look carefully if I wish to perceive His actions. I seek the dream's beginning because every time I see a "new thing" I sharpen my perception. Perhaps looking back will help me see the new things God does every day.

I retrace my steps past "1000.0" to a one-degree miracle. Looking back I see a winding path traced by a dream of which I wasn't yet aware. Just as the river doesn't appear imposing until it grows and assumes perceptible importance, this dream still trickled along as an apparently unimportant stream. No one, including me, saw it or recognized what it might become.

Just as the river originated before it looked like a river, so this dream began long before it could be recognized as a dream. *Inceptum Somnii*—the beginning of the dream—occurred on a chilly, cloudy day on a suburban neighborhood street. God performed a nearly imperceptible one-degree miracle and set me on a trickle of a path that eventually became a big dream.

I think that's how it usually happens. He begins with the equivalent of a single drop of water at just the right time and place. And if we listen and trust and persevere, a tiny drop becomes a stream and then a river.

So I'll place my sign at the moment of a one-degree miracle, but it's as artificial as the man-made rock wall at Lake Itasca.

It wasn't a dream ... and then it was.

Don't allow your resources to determine your vision. ▮

part 2

the journey begins

5 great mississippi river road

Dreaming is great, but at some point you have to start.

Twelve years after *Inceptum Somnii*, the dream had taken shape. The journey was underway.

Monte and I reached the visitor center. We were eager to get on the road, but had to wait for Becky, Steve, and Mark to walk up the six-hundred-yard path. We impatiently circled the parking lot a couple of times until our companions finally appeared and took forever with helmets, bike shoes, and last-minute adjustments. Everyone grinned and laughed and celebrated.

I felt terrified. I stared straight into the face of a fifteen-hundred-mile journey. I'd never done forty miles in a single day—ever! To complete this project I would have to ride nearly forty miles per day for forty days.

I wasn't ready. I don't think you're ever ready to follow a God-sized dream. You can always find reasons to wait a little longer. The perfect time never arrives. At some point you have to decide, because the only way to get started is to start.

It's difficult to pinpoint precise thoughts as we rolled out of Lake Itasca State Park and saw the initial sign proclaiming Great Mississippi River Road. Traveling north to begin a long southern journey felt strange, but we'd studied the map carefully. The road to Bemidji ("the first city on the Mississippi") took us mostly west and a few miles north. From there we'd head primarily south.

I made one commitment to myself before we began. I envisioned and imagined this dream for years, trained and prepared and prayed. I wanted to do my absolute best to not wish away a single mile. I didn't want to look past any day's ride to the next week, the next big speaking gig, or the finish line. I knew eight weeks would pass much too quickly, and I wanted to savor and appreciate each day. So as Mark, Steve, Becky, Monte, and I rolled toward our first turn, I didn't want to think about fifteen hundred miles and the finish line in New Orleans. I didn't want to visualize our Day 1 destination in Bemidji. I just wanted to crank along and appreciate a ride with friends on a beautiful morning.

All of us planned to do three or four miles together, about Monte's daily mileage limit, as sort of a grand commencement parade. When Monte got tired he jumped into the empty "kid-carrier" Becky towed behind her bike. Mark and I kept going; Steve waited to help Becky get organized. She intended to catch up, ride a bit farther, and then head back to pick up the trailer. Things didn't quite go according to plan.

Apparently Monte wasn't too keen on the idea of riding in the kid-carrier. As they coasted down a hill, a car passed. He spooked and jumped out, sending himself, the carrier, Becky's bike, and Becky tumbling into the ditch.

Thankfully, after a few scary moments, Steve concluded no serious injuries had occurred. Becky had some nasty-looking road rash, but they'd dodged disaster. At this point Mark's cell phone buzzed and we discovered what had happened behind us. He turned back to help while I kept cranking, chuckling at the notion that Monte nearly derailed our epic expedition after five miles.

Steve caught up and reported Becky was a bit scraped and bruised but otherwise okay. Then Becky, Monte, and the trailer appeared. Finally, Mark huffed and puffed his way back into the fold. As we rested and reflected on catastrophe averted, Steve asked if I'd reset my odometer back at the lake. We were fourteen miles into our journey.

He laughed. "Cool. One more mile and you'll be 1 percent of the way." Somehow, his bit of math wasn't much comfort.

Mark, Becky, and I completed Day 1 rather routinely. Steve received a phone call and had to turn back to prepare for an unexpected meeting, so he wasn't able to complete the ride to Bemidji as we'd hoped. Otherwise, the remainder of the first day passed uneventfully.

We crossed the Mississippi three times during the first day. It was a bit disappointing. Even thirty miles from its source, the great river offers little clue of its eventual magnitude. It's nothing more than an ordinary-looking stream, no different from dozens of similar waterways in northern Minnesota.

It was impossible to judge by initial appearance which would disappear completely and which might combine with others to form important tributaries. Road signs placed by those who already knew the outcome provided the sole clue that this particular creek formed the genesis of one of the world's great rivers.

Henry Schoolcraft started his search farther downstream, where the result was obvious. Here, still so close to its birth, there's simply no way to know which stream will survive and grow until it literally alters the map and spawns an entirely new culture along its shores.

Like the river, dreams look mostly alike at the beginning. There's no knowing which will fail, which will succeed, and which will become Apple or Microsoft. Some unfathomable, unpredictable confluence of circumstance, talent, passion, tenacity, and providence arrives at a specific point in time.

It's easy to look back and pretend the wildly successful dreams were inevitable. You look at Google or Facebook today, Ford or GE a century ago, and it's hard to imagine the world without them. Their wild, off-the-charts success changed everything, and it's easy to observe from downstream and believe the results were obvious from the beginning. They weren't.

At the beginning they appeared no different from thousands of other apparently crazy notions. Others can speculate about specifics and analyze what differentiated this enterprise from all the others. Mostly I think it's an unproductive search for a shortcut, a magic bullet. So we invent a formula, sell it for $19.95, and write books and get paid to speak about it.

But the silver bullet doesn't exist. Excellence and success rest on timeless principles. Every "overnight success" stems from hundreds of small choices and a whole bunch of hard work, commitment, and sacrifice. But one thing's for sure: The originators of those huge successes didn't quit. Even when their ideas didn't seem to be going anywhere, when others said they were crazy, when objective analysis might have told them to surrender or change course, they stuck with it because it was a dream. Dreamers believe they can change the world, which doesn't always make objective sense, initially. The long road to "amazing" usually begins at "crazy."

The message, I think, is not to give up on dreams too soon. I wonder how many amazing ideas have died simply because someone looked at them in their infancy and decided they could never amount to anything.

A dream is an all-in affair. You have to believe enough to see it through. It may die anyway, for any number of reasons. But you can't know at the beginning how it'll play out, any more than you can predict from initial appearance which stream will become the mightiest river in North America.

Dreaming is risky business. You can't tell which stream will become a great river, or which dream will change the world, unless you're willing to embrace the risk and head downstream as far as the dream will take you.

And even more important: You never know the end result of your actions. The apparently doomed stream actually feeds into a larger waterway. In the same way, your efforts aren't wasted, because God causes all things to work together for good (Romans 8:28). If you're following a God-inspired dream, He won't waste your efforts or your struggle. When God's involved, what seems like a failure—isn't.

One thing's certain, though. The dream's invitation won't lead anywhere until you decide to follow.

Dreaming is great, but at some point you have to start.

6 paul bunyan's shadow

Our lives are filled with the mystery and wonder of God-inspired serendipity.

Paul Bunyan and Babe the Blue Ox greeted us at the shore of Lake Bemidji. An eighteen-foot-tall pipe-smoking lumberjack and a colossal blue ox put things back in perspective following the shock of Becky's crash. We munched sandwiches between Paul's gigantic boots and debated whether the width of Babe's horns matched the legendary dimensions of "forty-two ax handles and a plug of chewing tobacco."

Completing Day 1 seemed like a monumental accomplishment, but we lacked an appropriate commemoration of an important milestone. Staged photo ops and press conferences create the impression that any noteworthy event automatically attracts herds of photographers and adoring admirers. No one seemed to notice Mark, Becky, Monte, and me as we snapped a few photos with Paul and Babe in blustery, deteriorating weather.

A woman approached, greeted us, and introduced herself. "Hi, I'm Lori, and I'm president of the Bemidji Chamber of Commerce." She wanted to know our story, apparently curious about bike jerseys, dog, trailer, and handcycle. Becky located a business card and explained our mission, and a complete stranger became an instant, enthusiastic project supporter. She made phone calls, and a newspaper reporter/photographer appeared. Becky's phone rang during our interview, and we had an appointment with a television crew the following morning.

We thought we were supposed to be doing something special, but our very best choice was to simply be with each other and those goofy statues and enjoy the experience of the day. By not trying to create a phony event, something wonderful and personal occurred. And we had nothing to do with it other than just showing up.

Simple coincidence doesn't account for this occasion. I believe God played a role in a pivotal encounter. It wasn't mere chance, but I also believe God doesn't slide us around like pawns on a chessboard. Though I ponder the mysterious interplay between human freedom and the way God works for good within the events of our lives, I certainly don't claim to understand it. Mystery doesn't mean I know nothing; it simply means I don't know everything. I'm okay with that.

Rich's Ride gave me the priceless gift of time. Cranking along roads and trails, mostly alone, five or six hours each day afforded the wonderful luxury of time to wonder about mysteries and consider truths. How does God simultaneously allow evil, orchestrate good, and provide complete freedom of choice? It's a good question to wonder about when you're alone in quiet north woods.

My pastor friend Al Helder sat with me through a lot of tough questioning in a hospital room after my injury. Permanent paralysis gets you thinking about the mysteries of God's plan, and we spent countless hours talking about accidents, healing, suffering, and how God works for good in even the most difficult circumstances.

I recall how Al often gazed intently around a room and almost whispered, "Nobody's here by accident." When you realize you're in a room filled with people who arrived from unique backgrounds along winding paths through an endless series of independent choices, and somehow your gathering's not accidental, "Nobody's here by accident" broadens perspective and raises questions for which we won't find answers on this side of eternity. Back roads provide a wonderful setting for that sort of reflection.

I think of episodes like our meeting in Paul Bunyan's shadow as incidents of God-inspired serendipity. Some might object because serendipity implies a happy accident. I don't believe our unexpected connection with Lori and Bemidji's Chamber of Commerce was an accident at all, but I'll choose to keep serendipity on the authority of a famous philosopher, Humpty Dumpty. In Lewis Carroll's *Through the Looking Glass*, the wise old egg explains his views on words and their meanings:

"When I use a word," Humpty Dumpty said, in rather a scornful tone, "it means just what I choose it to mean—neither more nor less."

"The question is," said Alice, "whether you can make words mean so many different things."

"The question is," said Humpty Dumpty, "which is to be master—that's all."

So I'll be the master of my own term. Words matter, and labels matter a lot because the label often becomes the idea in a sound-bite culture. Attaching a label to this sort of event opens doors to potential misunderstanding. But creating the label also spurs contemplation during long bike rides. Sometimes that kind of reflection leads to deeper, more refined understanding and the interesting opportunity to explain what you think you've learned.

God-inspired serendipity involves at least three elements. It's the experience of discovering something pleasant without specifically seeking it. It's not an on-demand occurrence. With advance notice, Lori might have garnered more attention with a prearranged press conference to memorialize the inaugural day's ride. But the more formalized and efficient moment might have lacked the sense of personal involvement and generosity. Lori wasn't simply doing her job. She became a friend and connected us with her friends both in town and down the road. Even with similar results the experience would have been altered, perhaps diminished, if it had been pre-scripted.

God-inspired serendipity requires an open mind and a willing, prepared heart. Events like our encounter in Bemidji are the result of God working in our lives, and we choose whether we're available and ready to see what's right in front of us. *See, I am doing a new thing! Now it springs up; do you not perceive it?*

Scientist Alexander Fleming once noticed an unintentionally uncovered Petri dish "contaminated" with an unknown mold.

Rather than lamenting his carelessness and discarding the spoiled experiment, Fleming's trained eye observed the absence of bacteria around the mold. His open mind and ability to look beyond preconceptions led directly to the development of penicillin. How many other important opportunities are missed or delayed because observers weren't open and ready to perceive the significance of an unanticipated event?

Louis Pasteur famously observed, "Chance favors the prepared mind." I'll modify his comment: God-inspired serendipity favors an open mind and a willing, prepared heart.

What I especially like about this notion is our active involvement. God's in control, but we're invited along on the journey of discovery. God always keeps His promises but rarely places His answers directly in our hands. Instead, He places them within our reach and offers to journey with us as we claim them. Like the unopened gift under a Christmas tree, we claim the promise by first perceiving and then unwrapping the gift.

So I think we're more likely to experience God-inspired serendipity when we're engaged in particular kinds of activities. Mark, Becky, and I weren't doing anything special, but we were doing it together. We chose to enjoy the experience of the day and our relationships with each other rather than obsessing on some specific task. By having fun we opened our hearts and perhaps conveyed an attitude that invited Lori to approach. We're wired for authentic relationships. When we honor people above time and tasks, we increase our ability to experience God-inspired serendipity.

We might better perceive this phenomenon through prayer, quiet time, and service, but I suspect the specific activity matters less than being open to God's Spirit guiding and speaking to us. I don't know how it works, exactly. In Paul Bunyan's shadow we experienced God-inspired serendipity, and this simple interaction exerted small-but-powerful influences on the remainder of the journey.

Lori walked back from an ordinary lunch, noticed our odd little gang, and stopped to investigate. She sensed the excitement and jumped in with offers of assistance. We made a new friend, landed some valuable media exposure, and left with a few great contacts in other towns along the route. The encounter planted seeds that took a while to germinate regarding our understanding of our overall mission and direction.

We also found out about the Paul Bunyan Trail.

Pat, the newspaper reporter, was a cyclist, so he had a special interest in our project. As we chatted he asked, "Are you looking forward to the Paul Bunyan Trail?" His matter-of-fact question implied everyone knew about the trail, and of course it was my intended route. My ignorance clearly astonished him. "You have to take the Paul Bunyan Trail!"

So we completed the interview and received directions to the trailhead. Mark packed his bike and headed home. Becky stowed our gear, and we headed off to check out the Paul Bunyan Trail.

At first sight, I wasn't impressed. We passed this supposedly major bikeway twice without spotting the obscure trail. I guess I expected some kind of important-looking marker at the beginning of a trail named after a larger-than-life legend. Instead, a nondescript blacktop path followed a side street before disappearing into dense woods. Babe's "forty-two ax handles and a plug of chewing tobacco" horns wouldn't have fit on Paul Bunyan's trail.

During our months of preparation I imagined having my day-to-day route entirely predetermined. I investigated Internet sites, emailed local bike shops, and contacted cycling clubs for advice and information. I apparently asked the wrong questions to the wrong people because I received spotty, inadequate responses. So I resigned myself to discovering the route as we traveled. I had some notion of the first week, but my sketchy plan dissolved with the reporter's directive. "You have to take the Paul Bunyan Trail!" How could I say no?

Perfect

My confidence wasn't exactly bolstered when Becky called Jamil, the TV reporter. "Paul Bunyan Trail? Yeah, I've heard about it, but I'm not exactly sure where it is. No worries, though. I'll find it."

No worries. Day 2 would begin with an early-morning television interview, and then Monte and I would follow the skinny blacktop ribbon into the woods. I imagined being hopelessly lost as bears chased me down a dead-end path to nowhere. My friend Rob Cowles joked before we left home that if a bear appeared I should be sure to get a picture ... at least I think he was joking.

Jamil appeared bright and early in her TV station SUV and unloaded her camera gear while Becky wrestled the handcycle from the trailer. Becky was stiff and sore, aftereffects of yesterday's crash, and the excitement of opening day had dissipated. We hadn't quite worked out a smooth system for loading and unloading. As I watched her struggle I began to understand the difficult daily grind she faced in the coming weeks.

We completed our interview, and Jamil offered to follow us for a few miles to get some action shots. Since the bike trail was a converted railroad route and didn't follow roads, she and Becky had to determine where they could drive to intersect the trail. So with some small bit of confidence that we'd eventually meet somewhere, Monte and I headed off into the forest.

After a couple of miles I realized I owed Lori and the newspaper reporter an enormous thank-you. This nearly invisible trail was perfect.

The Paul Bunyan Trail is a rails-to-trail project. A state government and nonprofit partnership bought an abandoned railroad line, ripped up the tracks, and paved the trail. The result is a beautiful pathway through small towns and pristine woods—no traffic except where the tracks crossed a road. Much of the trail literally felt like a tunnel through overhanging trees, which were just assuming autumn colors. Since railroads avoided steep grades, inclines were negligible.

The New Testament Greek word *teleios*, translated "perfect," means "full, needing nothing for completeness." *Teleios* implies being what's intended and completely fulfilling a purpose. As a way of getting my journey off to a positive, inspiring beginning, the Paul Bunyan Trail left absolutely nothing to be desired. It was perfect.

Since Monte trotted beside me in this forest wonderland, I cruised easily so he wouldn't tire too quickly. We didn't know where we'd stumble across Becky and TV lady Jamil, so I decided it was best to take it easy. No point in hurrying to complete a journey on a perfect trail.

Perfect is another word requiring careful use. For some the word connotes absolute freedom from flaws or defects. We're admonished against obsessive perfectionism. After all, nobody's perfect, right? Certainly this trail wasn't free from bumps and cracks. But remember the wisdom of Humpty Dumpty. We're masters of our words. And this trail was perfect in another sense.

The Paul Bunyan Trail was just what I needed on Day 2 of my ride. Away from traffic and noise, free from distractions, with negligible inclines and declines, I could slow my mind and take time to assimilate the remarkable reality of this project. We prepared, planned, publicized, and trained for more than six months. Attracting sponsors and supporters became all-consuming. Once we published the schedule, there wasn't much space for wondering whether we could actually pull it off.

Now we'd passed the hoopla and excitement of beginning. The reality of multiple forty-mile days on a handcycle rattled my brain like a Paul Bunyan footstep. I'd watched Becky struggle with the gear and the pain of her crash. Suddenly I felt totally unqualified to honor this enormous commitment.

I needed peace. I needed the confidence I'd gain from a smooth day of riding, knowing I could acknowledge and confront the fear and muster the courage to keep going. I knew this ride, like all worthwhile journeys, would present its share of obstacles and struggles. But on Day 2 I needed seclusion, simplicity, and success.

For my needs in a particular situation, the Paul Bunyan Trail was perfect. The previous day's God-inspired serendipity provided exactly what I needed in a completely unexpected manner.

About a half hour later the trail approached a crossing. Monte's ears perked up and he broke into a full run as he spotted Becky and Jamil waiting on the road. If I hadn't known better I'd swear he was showing off for the TV camera and making sure everyone knew he was the true star of the show.

We did more interview footage and a few more action shots. Monte's running day was done, so he jumped into the car. Another goodbye, and I cranked away from the crossing. The early morning's somber uncertainty dissipated as bright, sunny skies appeared. I attached my Go-Pro helmet camera and captured some of the glorious surroundings as I cruised around lakes past picturesque fishing resorts. For the next few hours I encountered Becky and Monte occasionally, but mostly I just cranked along steadily in peaceful solitude.

Two days and eighty-nine miles on the Paul Bunyan Trail helped me get mentally centered. I knew the rest of the ride wouldn't be so pristine, but for now it was a great opportunity to settle into the rhythm of long daily rides. The days and the trail were perfect.

The second day on Paul's trail did present one significant obstacle. About halfway through the morning I rounded a bend and had to jump on the brake. I'd wondered about bears and other critters, but I suddenly confronted an odd question: "If a tree falls in the woods and completely blocks the trail, does it make a sound?"

Okay, so I didn't really care about the sound, but I was stymied by the large tree in my path. No way to move it, nobody in sight, no U-turn. The path was much too narrow for my bike's eighteen-foot turning radius. I tried my cell phone to see if Becky might be nearby. No coverage. I was stuck with a single less-than-attractive solution.

I had to back up. And since there's no "reverse" gear, I had to push backward with my hands on the pavement. So I reached down and slowly inched back. I tried to recall when I last crossed a road, but I'd sort of gotten into a rhythm of cranking along without attending to details. The distance didn't matter anyway, because there wasn't another alternative. I had to just back up until I reached a crossing.

About a half mile of this awkward technique finally backed me onto a street. A gravel road paralleled the bike path, so I cranked past the fallen tree to the next intersection and rejoined the trail. Minor digression, problem solved, valuable lesson learned.

Adventures aren't scripted. Obstacles appear, but mostly they're diversions. It's best to accept them as part of the experience. Then you can concentrate on finding a way back to the trail and moving forward.

Our lives are filled with the mystery and wonder of God-inspired serendipity. ▮

coincidence, right?

God frequently orchestrates long-term arcs rather than sudden U-turns.

I don't understand how prayer works.

Others seem absolutely confident about the precise connections between prayers and answers, but mostly I'm not sure at all. I believe in prayer and its power. I believe in talking transparently to God and doing my best to listen. I believe God hears prayers and I absolutely believe He answers every single time. But I don't always hear or perceive those answers. I don't usually see an obvious, direct, straight-line connection from my prayers to subsequent events.

Frankly, I'm okay with not understanding. I don't believe everything positive represents a yes from God or that disappointment always signifies a no. God's orchestrating a much larger, longer-term story with a more complex web of characters and subplots than I can possibly imagine. His story never wavers and yet somehow incorporates our choices and mistakes and successes. I don't want to make the story artificially smaller just so I can pretend to understand.

Making prayer synthetically simplistic puts God in a human-created box. The dream of Rich's Ride didn't need a smaller, more predictable, more understandable version of God. A God-sized dream requires a God big enough to hold it in the hollow of His hands. One of the incredible gifts of hours cranking alone was the opportunity to contemplate God's incomprehensible majesty. And the more I tried to imagine Him, the more I knew I didn't really know. Like I said, I don't understand how prayer works.

Elk River Day

Friday of Week 1 was a late-start day. St. Cloud seemed determined to live up to its name as dense fog obscured cars in the hotel parking lot. I was committed to finishing the first week well, but I wasn't crazy enough to ride back roads in thirty-foot visibility with a silly little flag as my only alert to passing drivers.

So I rolled away from the hotel later than planned. Detours redirected my intended route and reminded me to embrace inevitable on-the-fly course adjustments. I tried to follow makeshift signs marking alternate roads as Becky scouted ahead for best options.

This Friday was one of many days on which Rich's Ride showed me I'm frequently oblivious to God's bigger story. While I worked around weather and roadblocks, God did a new thing. Bike riding became background for important events developing beyond my awareness. As I cranked along country roads through deep green Minnesota forests, He arranged an appointment and transformed this foggy Friday into a signature incident.

The hidden story line actually began weeks earlier when I published the initial draft of our itinerary. Our friend Kathleen Michie (who also happened to be one of my first physical therapists) noticed we'd be near Elk River, home of her close friend Kelley McGowan. So Kathleen invited Kelley to follow our progress on the Internet. She did much more.

When I rolled out of St. Cloud, Kelley tracked my progress via the GPS device that translated the bike's real-time location to our web page. As we meandered through the unintended twists and turns of our impromptu route, she realized I might literally ride within a few blocks of her house. She called Becky and asked if we were interested in meeting and sharing our story at a couple of last-minute gatherings. So while I pedaled along, blissfully unaware of behind-the-scenes developments, Kelley contacted friends in a couple of different groups. By the time Becky told me what was happening, she and Kelley had arranged two speaking gigs.

The day's ride had to be shortened a bit due to the foggy late start and our improvised afternoon meeting in a nearby park. As the sky cleared we ended the first week of riding, loaded the trailer, and headed off to talk with a group of home-school students and parents. I always recall this episode of the story as "Elk River Day," even though I later learned we actually stayed and spoke in the neighboring town of Otsego. No reason to let facts get in the way of a good memory.

Honestly, I didn't think kids in a park wanted to stop, sit quietly, and listen to me talk about a bike ride. I'd designed my presentation for a controlled indoor setting with PowerPoint visuals. But the kids—and their parents—actually seemed interested, curious, and especially fascinated by my odd bike. The kids asked lots of questions, mostly about Monte and the handcycle, and we enjoyed a relaxing, unrehearsed encounter that couldn't have been pre-scripted.

The theme of Elk River Day continued as the important stuff developed beyond my consciousness. Becky had been scrambling to revise our lodging plans. While I enjoyed my midday bike ride she searched for an affordable hotel near our evening speaking event at Kelley's church. As I finished my presentation and talked with individual kids and parents, I noticed Becky had gathered with a small group of moms. Obviously they were praying together.

The first week had been difficult for Becky. I got to ride a bike. She managed equipment and luggage, arranged lodging on the fly, fielded calls and emails, and orchestrated an evolving schedule. She also navigated and tried to keep track of my location so she could keep me fed and hydrated. In addition, she had to deal with me—no small chore—and help with dozens of small tasks inherent to life in a wheelchair away from our familiar home environment. She was still recovering from the first-day crash that left her a bit more banged up than she wanted to acknowledge. Her role as the entire on-the-road support team for the project proved to be more difficult and stressful than we'd anticipated.

Our preparations hadn't accounted for the cumulative effects of the myriad challenges she'd accepted, so when I saw Becky off to the side praying with a group of moms, I felt grateful for her moment of support and encouragement. And, as usual, I was oblivious to what really happened right in front of me.

See, I am doing a new thing!
Now it springs up; do you not perceive it?

My answer, sadly, is usually, "Oops, sorry, missed that one."

Becky told those women she hadn't been able to find nearby accommodations. They suggested a few options, including a hotel directly across the street from the church, but she'd already tried them. As Becky shared her frustration and apprehension, one lady said, "Why don't we pray about it?" So they stood together in the park, hand-in-hand, and talked to God about accumulated concerns, worries, and needs.

As her new friends helped Becky reload the trailer, we reviewed a great afternoon and made plans for the evening. One lady encouraged us to try the conveniently located hotel that already quoted a price far beyond our budget. Since I wasn't cranking the bike I drove to the hotel, but I still knew few details as I pulled into the parking lot and waited while Becky headed inside.

She was gone a long time. Finally she returned, slid into the passenger's seat, and pointed. "Park over there." Then she related the entire story, concluding with the hotel manager's offer of a suite for less than a third of the previously quoted single-room rate.

I don't understand exactly what happened. I know the events and circumstances, but I won't even speculate about how it all came together. I'm not sure it's as simple as A causes B causes C.

But I also don't think it was all just happy coincidence. I believe God was at work, doing a new thing, keeping His promise to provide.

Here's what I do know. Like most important events on the ride, it wasn't anything I did or caused. While I enjoyed the scenery, Becky scrambled and worked to find a solution. I was just a guy taking a bike ride along a mostly unplanned route from St. Cloud to Elk River, completely unaware that God was writing an amazing story using pretty ordinary circumstances.

Then some new friends gently reminded us we weren't in charge and this really wasn't our story. Kelley and her friends helped us refocus, relax, and remember who we claimed to trust. They reminded us, in the words of an old Christian adage, to "work like it depends on us and pray like it depends on God."

I don't understand how prayer works. I don't need to.

The first half of Elk River Day concluded.

I'll confess to feeling a bit apprehensive as we pulled into the nearly empty parking lot of Otsego's Christ Church later that evening. I wondered if anyone would show up on a Friday night, with almost no notice, to listen to someone they'd never heard of a day earlier. As folks arrived and we enjoyed warm greetings and friendly conversations, I was reminded that God would gather the people who needed to hear the story. Secretly, I also figured Kelley must be pretty persuasive.

As a physical therapist, Kelley was curious about the bike, my injury, and how we'd gotten to this point. We had quite a bit of fun at her expense as she attempted to pedal a handcycle around the sanctuary. I did my presentation and we enjoyed a wonderful discussion driven by sincere, challenging questions. As we talked afterward I was humbled when Kelley shared a small piece of her story.

In her early twenties she struggled through a tough battle with cancer. As she endured multiple rounds of chemotherapy and radiation treatments, Kelley talked to God about rearranging priorities regarding two issues.

When doctors offered gloomy predictions about a "low probability" of becoming pregnant, she wondered about future plans for a family. She accepted the reality that her desire for children might be fulfilled through adoption.

Kelley's physical capabilities had also changed. Prior to treatment her goal was to climb the "Colorado fourteeners," the fifty-eight Colorado mountain peaks that exceed fourteen thousand feet. But the cancer and side effects of treatment significantly limited her ability to breathe at high altitudes.

For a long time she couldn't run or even walk fast, and she had to redefine her priorities regarding exercise.

When we met on Elk River Day, sixteen years after the treatments ended, Kelley had just completed her first duathlon (run-bike-run). She beat her "dream time" by more than fifteen minutes, inspired by a personal cheering section including her husband and three young children (to whom she had given birth).

I'm still processing Kelley's concluding statement.

> *"I sincerely hope I never have to go through the cancer battle again, but I wouldn't trade my cancer experience for the world, because of how close to God I became and how much I learned to trust Him and depend on Him. I do think He possibly allowed the cancer to happen to get my attention, and I'm thankful for that "wake-up call." It rearranged my priorities. Definitely it was worth it for the relationship I now enjoy with Jesus."*

It was one of many moments on the trip when the only response I could muster was "Wow!"

I never seek to romanticize my injury; being confined to a wheelchair stinks. It's painful and frustrating and embarrassing, and I ask God regularly to heal my injury. I'm incredibly grateful for all the good He's brought from a tragic accident, but I can't say I'm thankful for the injury or its terrible consequences. And I absolutely do not believe God "caused" my suffering.

But Kelley's incredible testimony helped me reconsider. I am closer to Jesus because of my injury. I have learned to trust God a bit more. I still don't like sitting in a wheelchair, but those rewards are definitely worth any price.

I believe God answers prayers. He answered Kelley's prayers, and I believe He answered mine. In every way that really matters in Kingdom terms, God has healed me. He's used the circumstances of my injury to bless me in countless, unimaginable ways. I also believe God hears my prayers for physical healing. I don't know why I'm still paralyzed, but I emphatically reject the suggestion that God ignored my prayers.

As I said, I don't understand how prayer works.

Kelley talked about faithfully respecting God's timing. Maybe He told her to wait, or perhaps His yes involved the longer-than-expected time frame of a one-degree miracle. Maybe it took sixteen years to perceive the radical, but gradual, alteration that ultimately led her to a place of such great joy.

God works on an extended timeline. He promised a child to Abraham and Sarah when they were in their seventies, and they waited nearly twenty-five years for Isaac's birth. The Israelites entered the land of milk and honey more than six hundred years after God's promise to Abraham. Simeon served his entire life in the temple before he beheld the Messiah. God frequently orchestrates long-term arcs rather than sudden U-turns.

So if He doesn't seem to be responding, perhaps the answer isn't no or wait. Maybe He's doing the new thing we seek right now, but we need time and trust to see the fruits of His one-degree miracle from our limited perspective.

Kelley's story provided an opportunity to celebrate without analysis, to embrace the mystery of being held in the arms of a loving God whose ways and thoughts are beyond our comprehension. It was a chance to hang out with Jesus and a few of His friends, a reminder that Jesus is a Person rather than a collection of theological ideas. Hearing about Kelley's miracle helped me to know Him a little better and let go of knowing about Him.

Elk River Day was an implausible confluence of people, events, and circumstances. When I looked through the hotel window that morning at dense, impenetrable fog, I couldn't possibly have imagined the inspiring story of courage I encountered as the day concluded. When Kelley received that first phone call from our mutual friend Kathleen, she didn't know she'd open a Web page several weeks later and feel prompted to step into our journey in such a powerful way. When Becky struggled to make my daily ride as smooth as possible, she didn't visualize a supportive prayer circle of new friends who would help her rediscover personal peace.

Amazing coincidences?

God was at work doing a new thing, faithfully responding to spoken and unspoken prayers. I don't understand, but that's okay.

He's God. I'm not. I'm glad.

God frequently orchestrates long-term arcs rather than sudden U-turns. ▮

8 trajectories

Don't make choices based on fear.

And who knows but that you have come to your royal position for such a time as this? (Esther 4:14b)

Some of us are old enough to recall Apollo 13 as more than a blockbuster movie. When the enormous Saturn V rocket blasted off on April 11, 1970, spaceflight had become almost commonplace. The voyage toward a third manned moon landing appeared to be just another routine mission, but Apollo 13 reminded everyone that space exploration was anything but "routine."

A few hours after liftoff, an explosion ripped a gaping hole in the spacecraft and compromised critical life support, guidance, and propulsion systems. Moon landing plans evaporated as an inspiring adventure transformed into a desperate scramble for survival. I remember staring at our black-and-white television during the following days as an army of engineers and support personnel did about a million things at once to keep three astronauts alive and figure out how to return them safely to Earth.

Apollo missions included planned course corrections required to attain precise navigation targets. Computer guidance normally accomplished these complex adjustments automatically, but the blast destroyed those capabilities. As the crippled spaceship rounded the moon and began its return trip, Apollo 13 drifted off course. The exhausted crew would have to manually redirect their path following calculations relayed from ground personnel. Using untested methods and repurposed equipment, three men created a precisely calculated curved path toward an imaginary moving target thousands of miles away. Even a minor error would send them to their deaths.

I can't imagine how impossibly tiny a thirty-mile-wide reentry window must have seemed from such a vast distance.

Spacecraft and desired destination both moved at incredible speeds. The astronauts had to trust controllers' calculations and aim confidently at a precise empty spot in space. Their skillful maneuver established a complex trajectory that intersected almost perfectly with their minuscule moving target.

Blocking Traffic

During the second week of the journey, we were invited to address students at North Central University in downtown Minneapolis. When our host inquired about how I wanted to be introduced, I asked if we might have some fun. He smiled and nodded—a bit hesitantly—so I said, "Okay, don't introduce me at all. Introduce Monte, and then casually mention that Monte's owner came along."

So after some great music he said, "I'm about to do something I've never done in all my years as a pastor. I'm going to introduce a dog named Monte as today's presenter. Oh, by the way, Monte brought along his owner."

What a great way to hook a young audience. The students, of course, absolutely loved the idea of a dog in their chapel service. As I rolled onto the platform I stared into a sea of eight hundred excited young faces. Curious college students, a dog, the attention-grabbing handcycle, and the crazy story of this God-inspired ride created an ideal atmosphere for a message about hope, inspiration, and dreams.

At the end of the presentation students approached the stage and placed dollar bills and handfuls of coins near the bike to support Convoy of Hope. Their impromptu offering totaled nearly $600! As I soaked up their warm response and talked to individuals afterward, I could only hope they received some small fraction of the inspiration they gave me.

Afterward we had lunch with the university's administrators and absorbed more encouragement. By the time we packed the trailer and prepared to leave we were pumped about getting back on the road. As we pulled forward and stopped at a red light, a young man across the street waved and ran toward us. He motioned for me to lower my window.

"I was in chapel this morning, and I need to tell you a story." The light turned green, but he motioned for the folks behind us to wait. This was obviously important. Horns honked impatiently as he related his tale.

"Today is the first time I've been to chapel since school started. This summer I was diagnosed with a chronic illness, and I've been angry at God. Before this happened I was sure He'd called me to be a pastor, but now it seemed impossible. I actually considered not returning to school, but I didn't know what else to do. So I came back, but my heart wasn't in it. That's why I haven't been to chapel. I kept talking to Him, asking why, but I wasn't hearing any answers that made sense."

Horns continued to honk, but he was determined to finish.

"This morning I felt like I was supposed to go to chapel. I wasn't sure why, and I didn't really want to. But I showed up because I felt God's prompting.

"I had no idea you'd be there, but now I understand. God wanted me to hear your story. I've been feeling sorry for myself. I decided God couldn't use me, but your message turned my thinking around. God can use anyone, even a guy with this disease."

Moments like this remind me of Apollo 13's course correction. I picture trajectories converging in the tiny window of an urban intersection. I think of the apparently unrelated course corrections that brought me, Becky, and a particular young man to the same place and time. I try to imagine the choices made years earlier, the complex arcs of different lives leading to one specific appointment. It's reminiscent of the ill-fated Apollo mission, except much longer term with nearly infinite variables and moving parts.

I don't think it was accident or coincidence. I believe God brought all of those trajectories to a specific point in time to accomplish His purpose. I have no clue how that works. I know it's not the simplistic cause-and-effect process we so often imagine. He's God, I'm not, and I don't believe we experienced a chance encounter.

Weeks before the ride began we met with our core advisory group. As we wrapped up our discussion, Dick Foth prayed for people we would meet. He named specific individuals: a parent struggling with a disabled child, someone facing financial challenges, a young person searching for direction, a couple wondering about a collapsing marriage, a family facing grief or loss. He asked God to open and prepare their hearts and to arrange divine appointments in which they might be impacted.

Along the ride we met those individuals; this young man was one of them. God was doing a new thing in Minneapolis that morning. We didn't simply run into a kid at a random corner. At a downtown intersection, with irritated drivers waiting impatiently behind us, we showed up for a pre-ordained engagement.

That's how God works most of the time. He makes seemingly insignificant course corrections, one-degree miracles, sending us in long-term directions that don't make short-term sense. It's as if we're headed into empty space.

I can't begin to understand the complexities of this process. I don't know how God's omnipotence meshes with human freedom of choice or how He incorporates my mistakes, resistance, and feeble attempts at obedience into His plans. He's doing something like the Apollo 13 midcourse adjustment with infinitely more variables, creating incredibly complex trajectories to reach precise, eternally significant targets.

I'm glad God's in charge. I cannot possibly perceive the infinitely complex calculations of His cosmic calculus. I delude myself whenever I pretend I know how specific short-term events fit into God's eternal vision. An adage claims, "If you want to make God laugh, tell Him your plans." I suspect He chuckles even louder whenever I claim to fully understand the details of His plans.

It's not our job to shape events to conform to God's plans. He's already got that covered. His mission will be accomplished with or without our cooperation, but His desire always involves relationship. He wants us to experience the joy of walking along and being involved in building His kingdom. He doesn't need us. He chooses to invite us to perceive and follow a dream, to work with

Him and experience the fullness of fellowship with Him.

I think that's what happens as we do our best to listen and follow. He gently redirects us and sets us on trajectories guiding us to places He can use us. Of course we can't possibly see what He sees, so we try to draw straight lines and concoct simplistic short-term explanations to explain complex events.

Think of a time when you've found yourself in just the right place with just the right people in a setting no one could've anticipated, a time when something unexpected happened and changed lives in a powerful way. You know it didn't happen by accident. It was a divine appointment.

Imagine what brought those folks to a specific point, all the small decisions and twists and mistakes that placed them on trajectories intersecting in a tiny window of time and space. Imagine the endless course corrections, one small moment of each life building on thousands of others, all leading to an eternally significant interaction.

Divine appointments aren't always big-deal, traffic-halting events. Most occur routinely in coffee shops, church lobbies, workplaces, and family rooms. Teachers acknowledge a similar phenomenon called "teachable moments" when interest and opportunity collide. Great teachers treasure such events and strive to recognize them. They're complex and unpredictable, and when you spot one you interrupt whatever else was planned. You recognize a God-ordained moment in which long-term trajectories intersect in unanticipated opportunity.

These unplanned instances are holy ground, but I wonder how often we're too busy to notice or honor them. As a young man approached our car in downtown traffic, it would have been easy to obey the green light's command to pull away. I suppose the inconvenienced drivers saw our divine appointment as a rude, selfish, inconsiderate disruption. If I'd been one of them I likely would have agreed.

Discernment and wisdom highlight instances in which intersecting trajectories create a moment that justifies altered plans and commitments. Most conversations, even important ones, don't excuse ignoring traffic signals on busy streets. I don't know how I recognized an exception, but I'm certain the eternal implications of this particular interaction overshadowed momentary inconvenience.

In the Bible, Esther ascended to an influential position in a foreign land through a most unlikely series of events. She subsequently faced a difficult and potentially dangerous decision. Her uncle, Mordecai, encouraged her to overcome her fears and confront a volatile king on behalf of her people. *"And who knows but that you have come to your royal position for such a time as this?" (Esther 4:14b).*

Mordecai believed Esther faced a divine appointment as God worked through events in her life and placed her in a strategic position. God orchestrated a complex set of midcourse corrections and long-term trajectories "for such a time as this." She didn't arrange or anticipate an implausible set of circumstances. She could choose only whether to acknowledge and act on her unique opportunity.

That's our choice as well. God invites us to open our eyes and perceive the new thing He's doing in each of our lives. And He promises to walk with us as we confront the fear of interrupting safe, carefully constructed plans to keep His appointments.

Don't make choices based on fear. ∎

9 top of the hill

There's a top to every hill.

Some hills never end.

That, of course, is a lie. Even the longest, steepest hill leads to an eventual summit. The pain and struggle always conclude. You crank up a difficult ascent with faith and hope, with confident assurance that perseverance will be rewarded.

Cycling uphill is a pretty good metaphor for the difficult seasons of life. Everyone faces adversity—health challenges, grief, broken relationships, or financial struggles—and in those moments the enemy attacks with the illusion of an infinite, never-ending climb. Staring up an apparently endless incline is one of life's most discouraging experiences, because when you can't see the top it's easy to imagine it's really not there. What's the point of persevering toward an apparently nonexistent goal?

When there's no end in sight it's easy to give up, but faith provides this encouraging reality: *There's a top to every hill.*

Hello, Hills

The second week of Rich's Ride began in the southern suburbs of St. Paul. Chilly, gray drizzle greeted us at sunrise but gradually faded as we left the hotel and unloaded the bike beneath a service station's protective canopy. After a three-day weekend of speaking gigs and much-needed rest, I felt recharged and anxious to get moving.

We already knew the day promised a chance to practice our newfound commitment to flexibility. A spring flood had destroyed several bridges a few miles south, diverting all vehicles into a major highway construction project with narrowed lanes and no shoulders. Internet sites described cycling in this construction zone as “dangerous and strongly discouraged.” Maps didn’t indicate an obvious viable detour.

I met Becky about thirty minutes later where the road repairs began. While we discussed options a construction worker stopped his pickup and asked if we needed help. Becky explained our dilemma and asked if he knew of a safer alternative to this six-mile construction zone. He suggested the other side of the river and described an obscure route. We found a rickety old river bridge and crossed into Wisconsin.

Our personalized bypass led to a lightly traveled two-lane blacktop. Western Wisconsin greeted us with striking beauty, wonderful early fall colors, and quiet, peaceful surroundings. The road twisted through forests and orchards, providing great cycling scenery and light traffic. Only local vehicles bothered with the meandering route on the eastern side of the river. We accidently discovered a perfect route—except for one minor detail.

In Wisconsin, we met some serious hills.

These were different from the gradual, relatively infrequent ups and downs we encountered during the first week of the ride. The designers clearly didn’t consider my skinny arms when they created a lovely farm road that snaked along an unbroken succession of long, difficult climbs and exciting descents. It seems like descents should balance out climbs, since every uphill section led to a corresponding downhill. But it felt like I spent virtually the entire day climbing. I struggled with mental challenge and cumulative physical effects as one ascent followed on the heels of another.

To illustrate, I spent about fifteen minutes climbing one particular mile-long hill, then flew down the other side in three minutes. Repeating the same result ten times covers twenty miles—ten uphill and ten down—in three hours, with half an hour coasting downhill and two-and-a-half hours climbing. Though the route is equally up and down, it seems like you're crawling uphill most of the time—because you are!

I spent more than five hours of riding time to cover forty miles of hills. It was the toughest, longest day of cycling I'd ever done. But before this begins to sound like complaining, here's a blog excerpt:

> ***Becky waited as I crept slowly to the top of one especially difficult climb. "How was it?"***
> ***"It was tough." Then I smiled. "And I'm really glad we're here."***
> ***This is why we came. We didn't prepare and plan and train to do easy, flat trails. There's plenty of that at home. I could be sitting in an office, or staring at a ball game on TV. This is exactly where I want to be.***
> ***I feel great. We've been blessed with wonderful weather—though I wouldn't mind if the wind blew a little more from the north. We're working hard at something we believe in. We're touching hearts.***
> ***When you're fortunate enough to be in the middle of something like that, you don't mind a few hills.***

Sometimes life's like cycling in those Wisconsin hills. Some seasons feel like a continual grind up an endless ascent, but the endless part isn't true. Even when the summit's around the corner and you can't see it and you're discouraged and tempted to quit because you're certain the climb will never end, it's good to remember, in cycling and in life, there's a top to every hill.

I stated this principle once while speaking at a retreat. Afterward Eric approached and asked, "What about my wife's terminal cancer? There's no top to that hill."

This guy was hurting. On a deck beneath a million stars we spent a long time talking about fear and loss and apparently endless pain. Eventually we returned to the question about hills and his thoughts about death and endings and beginnings.

"I know the hill isn't endless for her. She'll reach the top, the pain will end, and she'll spend eternity with Jesus." He smiled at his mental picture, then began to cry. "I know it sounds selfish, but what about me? I have to go on without her. The end of her hill just means a harder one for me."

Selfish? Eric foresaw a terrifying emptiness, a hole in his heart, a hill he didn't want to climb forever. It wasn't the place for hollow assurances about temporary grief. In the dark stillness of a Colorado night, "the rest of his life" was an interminable, impossible mountain.

Except ... as he shared his fears he realized his horrific hill wasn't endless because we both believe all of life is just a beginning. He realized there was an end to even this terrible climb. He started to talk from God's eternal perspective: There's a top to every hill.

Climbs are a valuable part of the ride. I'm tempted to imagine the obvious pleasures of a route without ascents—speed without effort and gain without pain. Why can't cycling consist solely of exhilarating descents?

On that western Wisconsin day I cranked through spectacular surroundings past idyllic farms and lush woods hinting at changing fall colors. But zooming downhill, I hardly noticed. Blasting along at thirty miles per hour with my backside four inches off the ground, I had to concentrate on the road. There wasn't much opportunity to check out the scenery.

I noticed the beauty during the slow, difficult climbs. I still struggled, but there's a significant difference between welcoming the difficulty and appreciating the opportunities it provides. A friend once reminded me, "Life ain't all about bein' easy."

Downhill's the more dangerous part of the ride—and perhaps of life. Speed increases the potential consequences of a mistake. Easy incites a wandering mind, precisely when focus is most essential. A smooth road tempts you to coast and lose sight of the prize. Too much unearned progress creates a sense of entitlement and makes the next climb even harder.

rich's ride *By Rich Dixon*

Consider it pure joy, my brothers and sisters, whenever you face trials of many kinds, because you know that the testing of your faith produces perseverance. Let perseverance finish its work so that you may be mature and complete, not lacking anything. (James 1:2–4)

The hills are a gift. You have to learn to appreciate and embrace all parts of the ride. I still don't enjoy or look forward to cranking up long, challenging ascents. But I understand they're part of the journey for a reason. Greater challenge offers greater opportunity to grow and develop.

Nobody gets stronger riding downhill. Pressure and resistance enhance mental and physical toughness and endurance. Challenge fosters character and courage. "All downhill" sounds fun, but there's a certain shallowness to a life filled with hollow thrills devoid of authentic, earned achievement. Greater challenge offers greater opportunity. The hills of western Wisconsin offered just about all the opportunity I could handle.

There's a top to every hill.

notes

10 ride, rich, ride

Don't let what you can't do keep you from doing what you can do.

This is what the kingdom of God is like. A man scatters seed on the ground. Night and day, whether he sleeps or gets up, the seed sprouts and grows, though he does not know how. All by itself the soil produces grain. (Mark 4:26–28)

La Crosse, Wisconsin, was a lot of fun. Like Elk River Day, La Crosse reminded us God was at work on levels and in places we couldn't perceive.

We were invited to speak at a local high school. This opportunity reminded me again of how much I love interacting with kids. Once a teacher, always a teacher, and these students were a wonderful audience.

In La Crosse we also received a lot of media attention. Over a two-day span our project was featured on television, radio, and in the newspaper. As a result, lots of people knew what we were doing and recognized the bike and the trailer. We felt like minor local celebrities as we prepared to head south.

Our hotel was in the heart of the city. I discovered a manageable route along a bike path leading to the edge of town, but as we unloaded the trailer we encountered an unexpected complication: Octoberfest. Downtown streets were closed to traffic for the annual parade, so car and trailer weren't moving for a couple of hours. I could escape on sidewalks, but Becky was temporarily trapped. She and Monte had some extra time to relax and enjoy the parade.

As usual, I meandered through town a bit before finding the bike path. I even had to swallow male pride and ask for directions, but eventually I located a trail through parks and neighborhoods linking with a truly beautiful stretch of road.

This busy highway paralleled the Wisconsin side of the Mississippi River, separated from the water by railroad tracks. As the morning brightened, the river buzzed with activity. I watched tugs pushing heavily loaded barges and marveled at bald eagles soaring along bluffs towering above the road. A nice, wide road shoulder provided plenty of separation from cars and trucks speeding past, and dealing with traffic was a small sacrifice compared to the beauty of the surroundings. This was one of the rare spots when the road provided long stretches of uninterrupted river views, and miles melted away as I surveyed a postcard scene.

Honking horns and waving drivers startled me at first. After a few miles a cyclist pulled out of a driveway. "I've been waiting for you. Mind if I ride along?" He'd just wanted to ride a mile or two to honor our efforts. I realized what was happening. This guy, and all of those drivers, recognized the odd-looking bright yellow handcycle from the media coverage.

I felt a little like Forrest Gump, and I kept waiting for someone to yell, "Ride, Rich, Ride!" It never happened, but as I cranked along my spirit was buoyed by smiles, waves, and tooting horns. I hope those people realized the power of their small acts of encouragement.

About twenty miles later the trailer zoomed past. I rolled to a stop and listened as Becky recounted the fun of the Octoberfest parade. As always, Monte attracted lots of attention, and it's not every day you get to sit on a curb next to a man in lederhosen who is drinking beer at nine o'clock in the morning.

The remainder of the day's ride passed uneventfully. Warm temperatures, beautiful river views, and friendly supporters made this a pleasant, memorable road. People smiled and waved from front yards and along sidewalks in small river communities. And all along the way a beautifully poignant story unfolded just beyond my perception.

We'd arranged to end the day in one of numerous towns along the shore. I cranked onto the main street and saw the trailer. Becky waited inside the car, which was unusual, but I didn't think much about it until she emerged and walked quickly toward me. She appeared anxious.

"See that man?" I turned and saw him watching from across the street. "He's been following me most of the day. Every time I stopped I noticed his truck. At first I thought I was being paranoid, but it's the same guy and the same truck."

Becky had apparently attracted a stalker.

I still had to climb off the bike, so we couldn't just jump in the car. We were in the center of this village, but your mind invents horrible possibilities when you're pursued by a stranger in unfamiliar surroundings. So I was more than a little concerned when the man crossed the street and walked toward us. I briefly considered having Becky get Monte out of the car as protection, but his goofy, friendly face wasn't going to intimidate anyone. The man approached slowly.

As he reached our little staging area, he stopped and scuffed his feet and stared at the ground. He started to speak a couple of times, then hesitated. He wanted to begin a conversation but couldn't find the right words. He clearly didn't pose a threat, so Becky greeted him and broke the awkward silence. As he relaxed we listened to a heart-wrenching tale.

He saw our story on local television and drove to our planned route hoping for an opportunity to talk to us. He spotted me cranking along, then saw the trailer, but couldn't summon the courage to approach us. So he followed nearly forty miles searching for the right moment. When we finally stopped he stood for a long time because he didn't want to interrupt.

He wanted to tell us about his boy, who struggled with a rare and especially difficult form of diabetes. At age eleven, his son was beginning to understand the realities of his disease. He realized he wouldn't be able to participate in many of the same activities as his friends, and he was angry. His father didn't know how to talk to his son about their emotions. What he wanted to express—the reason he followed us all morning—was his appreciation for our story because it got them talking. A simple bike ride opened the door for dad and son to talk about overcoming a difficult situation.

He wanted to thank us for sharing the story of the ride, for the blog and the videos and Monte's weekly writing (yes, Monte contributed to the blog). He and his son looked at our website together and talked about how it's possible to do interesting, challenging things even with a disease or disability. It was the first time they'd been able to really talk about the disease and its effects, and they looked forward to following the rest of the ride together. This dad followed us all morning to tell us about his boy, to say thanks, and to shake our hands.

Then he turned and looked deep into my eyes. "It breaks my heart to see him so sad and angry. I just want to help him, but I don't know what to say." He pleaded for an answer. "What should I tell him?"

I don't know what's right in those moments, but I know it's not about words. This guy didn't chase us for hours thinking I somehow knew some magic words to fix an unfixable situation. He wanted to know someone understood. He needed the human connection of a handshake and a look in the eye. He knew there weren't any magic words for the difficult path he and his son faced together. He knew their problem wouldn't be solved, but he appreciated knowing it was shared.

"Tell him he's special," I said. "Tell him he's got gifts and talents and he can do whatever he wants with them. And keep telling him.

"Tell him not to let what he can't do keep him from doing what he can do."

He repeated the last line to himself. "Don't let what he can't do keep him from doing what he can do." He smiled, shook our hands again, and walked back to his truck.

During the next six weeks there were days I didn't feel like creating a blog post, days when I was tired or couldn't think of anything to write. Sometimes I wondered if it mattered, if anyone would care if I skipped a few days. I thought about an eleven-year-old kid and his dad. I thought about other people I hadn't met, who didn't or couldn't follow us for an entire morning. I realized the incredible blessing I received with each opportunity to share a small bit of this amazing experience.

This is what the kingdom of God is like. A man scatters seed on the ground. Night and day, whether he sleeps or gets up, the seed sprouts and grows, though he does not know how. All by itself the soil produces grain. (Mark 4:26–28)

I wonder how many opportunities we miss by insisting on our own notions of worthwhile outcomes, or how often we quit when seeds don't germinate immediately. Mostly we never fully appreciate the effects of our actions. Persevering, doing what's right, keeping commitments, and following the path—those are hard things when we can't see any immediate fruits from the effort and sacrifice. The important things don't happen overnight. Maybe that's why Jesus used so many planting analogies.

God used Rich's Ride to scatter seeds. He placed those seeds in the right lives and added fertilizer and water. Results from the ride sprouted and matured in places and ways we would never see. We needed to proceed with faith, hope, and love, trusting God to use our efforts even when we didn't understand the specifics. Knowing God's at work, and knowing He always works for good, has to be enough.

Don't let what you can't do keep you from doing what you can do. ▮

notes

11 peanuts and shells

Attitude matters more than circumstances.

Some days are peanuts. Some days are shells.

Most days, stuff happens. I can't always alter my circumstances, but my attitude determines how circumstances will impact me. I can choose those attitudes intentionally or allow circumstances to dictate.

Thursday of Week 3 began with a fresh sense of energy after a rest day in Davenport, Iowa. The route along the Illinois side of the Mississippi seemed promising—twenty miles to finish the Savannah-Rock Island trail, a short portage through some city traffic, and on to Muscatine, Iowa. The guy at the bike shop sounded absolutely confident and reassuring as he sketched the map. His certainty should have been my first clue.

The opening miles provided splendid early-morning river views and tours through suburban neighborhoods. The trail twisted through parks, along levees, and around riverside communities and resorts. Becky couldn't follow this convoluted path in the car, so I was on my own for the first part of the morning until I reached our prearranged halfway meeting spot in Rock Island.

The rain developed slowly. A light, almost pleasant drizzle became a wind-driven downpour as the path emerged onto an exposed levee. I found a picnic shelter in a small community park, and Becky and I chatted by phone as rain poured around me. Bike-shop-guy's sketchy map wasn't as helpful as we'd imagined. We laughed as we realized we were within a few blocks and couldn't locate each other. So much for GPS technology. Eventually the rain subsided and I resumed my journey toward Rock Island and an enticing patch of blue sky just down the road.

That cloudless spot remained tantalizingly close, apparently just on the opposite shore, while I cranked along in a constant sprinkle and a strong west wind. Peanuts or shells, this day was all about attitude. Suburbs melted into city, but according to bike-guy's map I still had a few miles of trail.

The "trail" quickly degenerated from a dedicated path to a series of narrow bike lanes on heavily traveled city streets. Our designated rally point was still a few miles away. Suddenly I was navigating city thoroughfares, roadside puddles, impatient city drivers, and construction zones. Seemed like every other block involved some sort of roadwork, and the first territory claimed by crews was the bike lanes. I merged with traffic several times, hoping texting teens and frazzled parents wouldn't miss my flag flapping in the breeze. After a few blocks dodging in and out of whizzing traffic and wondering which distracted driver would end my ride, the trail magically reappeared. I cruised along the shoreline, separated once again from cars, noise, and danger.

Around the bend, a temporary construction trailer blocked the path. Suddenly I sat in a jumble of trucks and heavy equipment. I was clearly in the way as contractor vehicles buzzed everywhere and workers in hardhats shuffled gear and equipment in all directions. I noticed a handful of orange-vested men digging around some unseen obstacle, so I called out, "Any idea where I go to reconnect with the bike trail?"

I just wanted to escape their work zone and find a way around the trailer. Seemed like a perfectly reasonable question, but I guess it came across differently to the man who started toward me, brandishing a shovel.

"You get your fancy #$%&-ing bike outta here or I'll show you a @$%#-ing trail." He hoisted the shovel like a baseball bat and suddenly I imagined my head might somehow resemble a hanging curve ball. I briefly considered pointing out that this was Illinois and he was probably a Cubs fan, which meant he'd most likely swing and miss. But he didn't look like he was in a joking mood and I wasn't interested in testing my bike helmet against the shovel, so

I figured it might be best to move along. I wandered through the confused mess of the construction site, ignoring irritated stares, until I rediscovered the trail.

As I cranked away and my heart rate subsided, I wondered why a stranger got so angry about an innocent request for directions. I was just trying to do something good, to live out this crazy dream, share hope with others, and raise some money for a worthy cause. What transformed him into a hardhat version of Babe Ruth threatening to smack me into the bleachers with his mud-caked bat?

I was a bit frustrated by a blocked trail, a hand-scrawled map, and a morning filled with minor, irritating interruptions. Every day I prayed for God's blessing, for a clear, safe route as I moved forward in pursuit of my God-sized dream. Hundreds of people covered my efforts with faithful prayers. So how could God answer those sincere prayers with a guy who cursed and threatened to knock me into center field? As I cranked away I remembered an important truth: It's not about me! The rest of the world's not focused on my dreams and goals.

My project wasn't the center of Babe Ruth's universe. His world was cold, dirty, hard work, and I was a guy in a fancy bike jersey on a goofy-looking tricycle who got to play around on a workday while he struggled to make a living. Maybe he was hung over, or his wife yelled at him as he left for work. Maybe he didn't know if he'd have a job once this project ended. Maybe he'd just had enough of people discounting his efforts.

Perhaps he prayed that morning for God to bless his work and allow others to understand and be a bit more tolerant and appreciative. Maybe he wondered about God's answer to his prayers as he stood ankle deep in mud, drenched by hours of rain, digging for who-knows-what to satisfy an impatient boss in the warm trailer. And perhaps he wondered why God would send a guy in a silly bike helmet and a spiffy yellow rain jacket on a weird-looking bike looking for a stupid trail.

Maybe construction guy was frustrated by a morning filled with minor, irritating interruptions, by people like me who perceived his work as "getting in the way" of their important activities. Who knows how many other cyclists had already complained because his hard work disrupted a bike ride?

Maybe he and I both wondered that morning about God's response to our prayers. Maybe we both needed to remember: It's not about me!

I hope I didn't seem impatient or irritated when I asked for help. Maybe I did, or maybe I didn't do anything wrong. Most likely this was simply a guy frustrated with a cold, miserable day, and this interaction wasn't my fault at all. But at the time I didn't try to see life from his boots. I wanted to get where I wanted to go, and this trailer blocked my path. This construction project at the center of their world was an obstacle to me.

Peanuts or shells.

If he prayed, he joined me in hoping God would honor our prayers. I believe God did, but I also believe He answers from a broader perspective I can't imagine. I need to trust that He sees what I can't.

I need to remember: It's not about me.

I'm just glad Babe Ruth didn't decide to use my head for batting practice.

Eventually Becky, Monte, and I met at the end of the bike route. We loaded the trailer, grabbed lunch, and drove through city traffic. As we unloaded again, the sky cleared and the west wind intensified. We planned another twenty miles along bike-shop-guy's recommended route into Muscatine. Two unexpected factors altered our plans.

The narrow, two-lane road provided absolutely no shoulder. Even at the extreme right edge of the highway I was completely exposed to traffic on this winding, hilly road. Becky had to drive behind me with flashers blinking, which protected me but made her an obstacle. I cranked along, constantly hoping some distracted country driver wouldn't rear-end the trailer. It wasn't much fun, but after just a few minutes things got worse. The road turned and pointed due west. I struggled directly into a forty-mile-per-hour headwind. In the discussion of peanuts and shells, the world was suddenly all shells.

Cycling into a nasty headwind is more discouraging than even the most difficult hills, because the wind typically lasts a lot longer than any hill. I was determined to complete the day's planned distance, so Becky crawled along behind while I struggled against the wind. Lines of vehicles backed up behind us, then passed with annoyed glares. I tried to put my head down and just keep pedaling, but I wasn't having much fun.

We topped a rise and faced a fairly long, steep descent. I stopped cranking, relieved to coast downhill for a few moments. But when I stopped pedaling the bike rolled to a complete stop! The wind stopped me dead on a steep decline.

I looked back at Becky. Her laughter convinced me we'd done enough. The day was finished. I rolled to the bottom of the hill and found a spot to pull off the road. We loaded the gear and concluded the shortest ride of the entire trip.

Some days are peanuts. Some days are shells.

Attitude matters more than circumstances.

notes

12 anschutz hill

God values character more than comfort.
Great obstacles create great opportunity.

Anschutz Hill captured the essence of Rich's Ride. In many ways it symbolized what the ride represented—the spirit, vision, passion, and sense of community that inspired and drove the entire project. But I'm skipping ahead. The story of Anschutz Hill requires a bit of context.

Week 4 of Rich's Ride started in Burlington, Iowa, after a weekend of rest and some wonderful Iowa hospitality. Our friends Glenn and Judy Bruckhart drove from Denver so Glenn could ride a few days, and I looked forward to his company. Glenn's a fellow retired math teacher and an avid cyclist, and I knew our conversation would wander to a variety of topics. With a bit of luck we just might solve the world's problems in three days.

Our planned route included stretches of lightly traveled riverside roads and some less idyllic highway miles. "Planned" isn't really the right word. We decided to explore a bit and try some back roads (they looked promising on the map), figuring we couldn't get too far off track as long as we headed generally south. It sounded good as we talked in the hotel parking lot.

The first part of the ride was fairly uneventful. After about ten miles of quiet back roads we endured a stretch of heavy highway traffic. Most folks think initially about the physical danger of cycling on the shoulder of a busy thoroughfare. I'll admit there's something a bit disconcerting about huge trucks rushing past at highway speeds, but perhaps the most disruptive part of highway riding is the traffic noise.

It's sort of in the background and you don't really notice it until you do. Then you realize the noise itself creates a sense of constant low-level anxiety. I think we get accustomed to background noise and aren't conscious of its effects. Seems like there's always traffic or music or chatter surrounding us, and we forget what quiet feels like. But after a few long days on peaceful country lanes and trails, the noise slaps you right in the face.

The traffic also forced Glenn and me to ride single file, curtailing our wide-ranging philosophical discussion. Fortunately we discovered an alternate route about forty-five minutes later and escaped the clamor of the major road. We gladly accepted a longer distance and a few extra hills in exchange for a peaceful, scenic road into Fort Madison to meet Becky and Judy for lunch.

Our original vision involved following the same busy highway out of town, but we agreed we needed another option. So we did a bit of lunchtime investigating and discovered what seemed like a promising alternative. Unfortunately, all roads look alike on those tiny cell phone maps.

It began well. Across the main road, winding through back streets and commercial areas, and out of town on a quiet two-lane farm road—this was exactly what we wanted. After a few minutes, the pavement turned to gravel. Now what?

I faced this dilemma a few times. You can retrace your path, but then you're either back to the heavy traffic or another alternate that might be as bad, or worse, than this one. And who knows, the gravel might end right over the next hill. Of course the road might end, too, but you don't think about that.

My bike wasn't designed for gravel roads. With skinny, one-inch road tires and an extremely stiff frame to increase efficiency, it's great for smooth pavement but not so comfortable when the surface gets rough. My body jarred with every small rock and bump and rut. As we topped hill after hill the gravel became less compacted, creating traction issues for my front-wheel-drive machine with most of its weight centered on the back wheels.

We bumped along for an hour or so. Finally we spotted an

intersection ahead, and laughed as we realized our "shortcut" had guided us right back to the highway we tried to avoid. However, life's all about perspective. Traffic was better than gravel, so we turned onto the busy four-lane.

After a few minutes we encountered Becky, Judy, and Monte at a convenience store. They'd been searching for us. We couldn't explain our route, since we weren't precisely sure where we'd been even when we were there. Becky told us she'd scheduled a meeting with media folks in Keokuk, then she and Judy left in search of a safer route. Glenn and I cranked along, cringing a bit each time a tractor-trailer buzzed past. About an hour later we spotted our advance scouts waving from the opposite side of the highway. They pointed us toward River Road.

According to the newspaper lady, River Road would be the perfect end to our cycling day. She promised a fifteen-mile cruise through gorgeous fall colors, ending in Rand Park at the iconic statue of Chief Keokuk.

She didn't mention Anschutz Hill.

She was right about this road. Quiet, lightly traveled, right on the Mississippi River bank, with a couple of challenging inclines to bluffs offering magnificent river views, this route was a cyclist's dream come true. After a few miles, we found Becky and Monte (Judy went ahead to check out campgrounds) in the tiny town of Montrose, Iowa. We met their new friend, who happened to operate an ice cream shop.

Long-distance cycling burns huge amounts of calories. You need to replace those calories, so you can eat just about anything in sight, guilt-free. After cranking forty miles on a warm late-summer day, thoughts of traffic noise and gravel roads faded at the prospect of an old-fashioned, handmade chocolate milkshake.

Cycling and life aren't all fun and glamour. A lot of it is just hard work, completing the miles in less-than-ideal conditions. If you expect a constant stream of roses and rainbows you'll be consistently disappointed. You deal with noisy traffic and gravel roads. You get lost. And you have to embrace those miles as an inevitable part of the journey. You learn to enjoy and even appreciate the tough stretches for their challenges and lessons.

You also learn that painful hills and dangerous turns fade in the light of a chocolate milkshake moment. You sit in cool shade and savor an unexpected treat. If you're lucky, you're aware enough to realize you hardly recall the details of the difficult ride that got you to this peaceful, delicious moment.

A few folks gathered. Small towns have their own informal communication system, and our arrival was an event. We told our story and complimented their isolated little oasis. They told us about the beauty of our remaining miles. And still, nobody mentioned Anschutz Hill.

We finished the milkshakes, waved goodbye to new friends, and headed off to meet Chief Keokuk. After a few minutes the trailer passed and Glenn and I chuckled as Monte stuck his head out the window and his ears flopped in the wind. We felt revived, refreshed, and ready to crank the final ten miles of the day along this beautiful secluded lane. Boats and barges on the river, almost no traffic in cool afternoon shade beneath the trees—hard to imagine a better setting.

The trailer reappeared. Becky shouted through the car window. "I think you should stop and let me drive you the rest of the way."

"Why? It's only three or four miles to the statue, right?"

"Yeah, but there's a really nasty hill."

We'd encountered some tough hills in three weeks of riding, and this was the first time she suggested stopping rather than even trying a climb.

"It can't be that bad."

She was adamant. "This hill is really steep. I don't think you should keep going."

We went back and forth a few times, and I was tempted. If it really was as steep as she claimed ...

"I'm not quitting. I'm going to give it a try."

So Becky shook her head in frustration and drove off, disappearing around the corner. A moment later, Glenn and I rounded the same corner and encountered the beginning of Anschutz Hill.

The road wound back and forth along the side of a bluff. Each corner promised the top of the hill but instead revealed an even steeper rise. The climb became increasingly difficult, and a quick check of my odometer showed we still had more than a mile to go. I began to understand Becky's warning. Using my bike's easiest gear I struggled just to keep moving.

Finally I had to stop and rest. I can't get off the bike, so "resting" on a hill involves locking my elbows to avoid rolling backward. Getting started again required a lot of extra effort, and I knew I'd be in stop-and-go mode until I reached the top. Crank a few feet, rest, crank a bit more. It was slow going. Each corner revealed a stunning river view and another bend in the road.

Finally! Around one last turn I saw Becky and the chief's statue. The slope increased one final bit, but with the goal in sight I couldn't quit. I crawled those last few yards, scarcely moving forward, until at last the bike rested at the top of the bluff.

I conquered Anschutz Hill. We sat together at Chief Keokuk's feet and gazed at a panoramic view of the river below. We saw the Keokuk Lock and Dam and the highway bridge to Illinois. The reporter appeared and we enjoyed a great conversation.

One of the ride's iconic images captures my final climb to the top of Anschutz Hill. The photo symbolizes important aspects of the ride.

I climbed a three-mile-long hill. I probably should have heeded Becky's warning and stopped at the bottom, but I'm glad I didn't. After cranking nearly fifty miles, I didn't quit. I faced the fear and overcame an extremely difficult obstacle. I'm proud of my accomplishment.

But my ascent of a difficult obstacle wrote a small chapter in a much bigger story. I wouldn't have had the opportunity to face such an important hurdle without the prayers, encouragement, and support of a huge circle of friends. I climbed the hill, but those folks got me to the base and gave me the confidence to try.

Hope is a confident expectation rooted in faith, and hope changes what's possible. In 1988, about five weeks after my injury, I sat on a smooth tile floor in my first wheelchair. I saw no hope in a broken body and a shattered life. Hopeless and helpless, I saw no possibility, no opportunity, and nothing worth living for.

I couldn't move ten feet.

Twenty-three years later I climbed a steep, three-mile-long hill. During those years God guided hundreds of people into my life, people who pushed and inspired and wouldn't accept *I can't* as an excuse. God worked through those people to transform tragedy into triumph, place me at the bottom of a difficult hill, and inspire the hope that allowed me to reach for an unattainable goal.

Hope changes what's possible.

Anschutz Hill was tough. I could've taken the easy way, the comfortable way. But you don't get stronger through easy and comfortable. The view from the top is a lot more satisfying when you work to get there.

God values character more than comfort.
Great obstacles create great opportunity. ∎

13 fill the bucket

Life is determined more by our commitments than by our feelings.

I knew this day would come. We planned for it, because we knew it was inevitable. You know it, too. You can't survive forever on determination and adrenaline. If you want to keep going long term, you have to refill the bucket.

I know myself well enough to know I get depleted if I don't recharge myself physically, mentally, emotionally, and spiritually. When we planned this project we inserted two rest days per week into our schedule. Those days were supposed to allow physical recovery as well as time to catch up on blogging, social media, and the unending logistical details. Unfortunately, for many reasons, things didn't always work out as we envisioned.

In the middle of Week 4 it all caught up with us.

We didn't expect it to happen on a rest day. We did a noon speaking engagement, then spent the rest of the day running errands and tending to minor tasks. When we finally reached our hotel in Bowling Green, Missouri, we still needed to update the blog, catch up on email, and plan the next day's route. Despite the "rest" day, I was tired and sore, and both Becky and I were feeling the cumulative effects of shortcutting our customary morning quiet time. Here's what I wrote in the blog:

> ***Our buckets are just about empty.***
> ***I'm not complaining. Tomorrow I get to take a bike ride—things could be a lot worse.***
> ***It's a lesson learned. If you want to travel well, you can't***

go full speed with no recovery time. That works in a short sprint, but life's a marathon. No matter how determined you are, you can't run a marathon on empty. If you want to travel well over the long term, you gotta refill the bucket.

It was a lesson we took seriously for the rest of the trip. Dream-following is a long-term commitment. It's important to train and prepare, but it's equally essential to refuel along the way. It's like plugging the phone into the charger each night. You need to replenish physical, emotional, mental, and spiritual reserves if you're going to follow your dream. You gotta refill the bucket.

So what happens when the bucket's empty and you wake up to a day of stuff to do? In an ideal world you'd anticipate and avoid the emptiness, but we don't follow dreams in an ideal world. So what do you do when you forgot to plug in the charger and the battery seems completely drained and you still need to get down the road?

First, you remember that "completely empty" is a lie. Our enemy encourages us to quit when the bucket feels empty, but we don't follow God-inspired dreams by ourselves. The dream began with Jesus' invitation, "Come. Follow Me." He travels with us and offers reserve power when ours seems drained.

I tried to remind myself each morning of the trip how blessed I was to have this opportunity, but on this particular morning I just wasn't feeling it. As I ate breakfast I tried to manufacture a positive attitude. My pretend optimism blew away in a fifteen-mile-per-hour south wind that meant an entire day battling a chilly headwind. I grumbled and griped and snapped at Becky a couple of times while she helped me get on the bike. As I pulled slowly away from the hotel I wondered if this might be the day I'd fail, crank a mile or two, and give up. Maybe the bucket was just too empty.

Five miles passed, then ten, then fifteen. By the time Becky caught up I'd done sixteen miles. Despite my apparent "empty bucket" I was actually having a decent ride. Our friend Scott Kissel left a voice mail on Becky's phone in response to the previous night's blog. He wanted us to know he was praying for us, and he reminded me I could lean on God's strength.

Scott's message provided a tangible reminder that we don't follow God-inspired dreams alone. Becky and I took a few minutes at the top of a hill in rural Missouri to talk about what it meant to be together on a journey of hope. We talked about Hebrews 12:1: *Therefore, since we are surrounded by such a great cloud of witnesses, let us throw off everything that hinders and the sin that so easily entangles. And let us run with perseverance the race marked out for us.*

On a day when our buckets felt so empty, it was good to be reminded that Jesus and His people walked with us. We knew we were surrounded by a great cloud of witnesses. We could draw strength from them. We felt their prayers and support. With that powerful assurance, you can keep going even when the bucket feels empty. By mid-afternoon I'd completed forty-three miles. It wasn't the prettiest or the fastest ride of the trip. It certainly wasn't the easiest. But I did it.

You've had those days. Every parent, spouse, student, employee, business owner, and dream follower knows about days when you don't feel like getting out of bed. You'd rather check out, but you don't. You made promises. People count on you. Your commitments matter more than your temporary feelings. So you show up.

As I cranked along I realized I liked what I was doing even though it wasn't easy or comfortable. This awareness seemed sort of odd until I remembered God-inspired dreams are more about character than comfort.

When President John F. Kennedy challenged America to send a man to the moon in 1960 he said, "We choose to go to the moon in this decade and do the other things, not because they are easy, but because they are hard."

I chose to do Rich's Ride not because it was easy, but precisely because it was hard. And when something's hard and uncomfortable, you're going to have days when you'd rather watch TV. But you don't, because life is long term and dreams matter. So you set your feelings aside. You show up.

Earlier I asked what happens when you wake up to a day of dream-following and the bucket feels empty. My first answer was to understand "completely empty" is a lie because we're not following the dream alone. We get to draw strength from Jesus and the great cloud of witnesses around us.

But we also need to remember the empty feeling isn't permanent and we know where to go to get the bucket refilled. Such knowledge inspires the kind of hope that can get you through a tough day.

Life is determined more by our commitments than by our feelings.

14 chain of rocks

Stop planning. Start preparing.

I looked forward to Old Chain of Rocks Bridge before the ride even began. An Internet search for scenic riverfront routes returned surprisingly few options, but an intriguing web page convinced me I didn't want to miss the St. Louis Riverfront Trail and its Mississippi River crossing at Old Chain of Rocks Bridge. However, like many preplanned episodes of the trip, reaching this historic landmark wasn't as simple as I imagined.

Saturday in St. Louis was a rest day. We stayed downtown directly across from the Gateway Arch, courtesy of our new friend Rich McClure, president of Unicorp. We used the opportunity to fill the bucket, unwind, explore downtown St. Louis, shop, and gawk with the other tourists at the arch.

Sunday morning brought a beautiful sunrise and a trip to a church in Alton, Illinois. We planned to speak there and ride the Illinois side of the river to a trail connected to Old Chain of Rocks Bridge. We had wonderful weather and a map with a clearly marked route. I'd do about thirty miles, cross the river, and complete the ride at the base of the arch. This afternoon cruise would spin my odometer past 750 miles and commemorate the halfway point of our epic journey. We'd sketched a great plan for a great day. We soon encountered another reminder to write our plans in pencil.

We learned to spend less time planning and more time preparing, because preparing is the key to flexibility. When you're well prepared you have options when a carefully constructed plan disintegrates. Preparation provides a foundation, depth, and background from which to approach and overcome inevitable unforeseen obstacles.

We enjoyed a wonderful morning in Alton. One amazing benefit of visiting and speaking in different churches is remembering Jesus doesn't live exclusively in your familiar building and worship culture. It's one of those things you say, but when you attend the same church with the same people every week it's easy to forget. People worship Jesus in an incredible variety of settings and styles. It's not about how or where we worship, but whom we worship. The folks in Alton were kind and welcoming and made us feel like part of the family. When you're away from home, dealing with stress and uncertainty, being adopted for a morning feels really good.

The road along the Illinois side of the river was as beautiful as advertised—a busy four-lane, lots of Sunday traffic, but nice, wide shoulders. The atmosphere was more hectic than usual because as I traveled south hundreds of cyclists pedaled north as part of a one-day century ride. Sunday drivers, cyclists, and everyone gazing at all the sights created a bit of a distracting, circus-type atmosphere. It was one of those stretches where I really enjoyed myself while Becky cringed with fear for my safety.

As I cranked along my attention was oddly diverted. As I watched the cyclists traveling in the opposite direction, I caught myself wondering who had the easier ride. I rode slightly downhill with the river, but into a significant breeze. They had the opposite conditions, and I wondered whether I'd rather ride downhill into the wind or uphill with it. Which was easier? As I realized what I was thinking, I thought about how silly the question seemed.

First, it didn't matter. I had my path and they had theirs. Wondering who had the easier task was absolutely pointless.

Second, easier isn't the purpose. If I wanted easy I could have stayed home and played video games. The goal is to travel well and appreciate my path. Four weeks had passed so quickly, and soon we'd be finished. I wanted to enjoy each moment of this amazing journey without wasting time on pointless speculation.

Finally, by focusing on someone else's task I looked to my left.

Meanwhile, a beautiful stretch of shining water passed unnoticed on my right. This was a scene I'd likely never see again, and I was missing it because I wondered about what someone else was doing.

This sort of comparing is simply wasteful activity. Its only function is taking attention from what's before me. It's really an excuse. As long as I'm concerned with someone else who might have more or less, I don't have to dig into my own work.

What matters isn't the other guy's path. What matters is moving forward toward my own goals. I need to discard whatever distracts me from following my dream.

About fifteen miles down the road I passed through a small town and connected to a trail along the top of a series of levees. The trail descended sharply every mile or so and then ascended again to accommodate a service road. It's actually a cool way to construct a trail system—mostly.

I cranked along the top of the levee, king of my world, enjoying the afternoon warmth. A sign indicated an approaching descent, so I slowed a bit and rolled over the edge. A specialized safety gate forced cyclists to dismount and walk through a sharp 120-degree turn. It was a simple and ingenious way to minimize intersection accidents, except the turn was too abrupt and narrow for the handcycle's long turning radius. Of course I didn't discover this fact until I was halfway through the gate.

I was hopelessly stuck. I tried rocking back and forth but got nowhere. Afternoon became late afternoon as I sat motionless, trapped by this "safety" gate. After about thirty minutes another cyclist appeared.

"Are you stuck?"

I'm amazed by the unintentionally stupid questions people ask and by my inclination to respond sarcastically. I resisted the impulse to claim I got trapped intentionally because I actually enjoyed the scenery and needed a break from riding my bike. The guy was really very kind and managed to free me from my trap. He also informed me there were two similar barriers waiting down the trail.

So I abandoned the bike path, found a busy road with practically no shoulder, and risked life and limb for a couple of miles. Finally I caught up with Becky, who couldn't figure out why I was riding in traffic when I had access to a perfectly good bike trail until I described the safety gates. She'd been watching on the GPS. "So that's why it looked like you were sitting in one place." Once more I resisted the urge to respond sarcastically. At least that's how I remember it.

Becky suggested it might be wise to pack up for the day and complete this ride in the morning. She was probably right. Afternoon was fading, and in diminishing light the path twisted through some trees and wasn't as easy to follow as our "well-marked" map indicated. But I was determined to complete my perfect plan, cross Old Chain of Rocks Bridge, and finish the day triumphantly at the Gateway Arch.

Determination is a good thing. Mostly. During the eight weeks of Rich's Ride I rarely feared actual physical danger. I was about to crank myself into one of those situations.

The levees wandered away from the main roads. In a few spots pavement turned to gravel and dirt, which made pedaling and following the path even harder. Finally I crossed a road I felt pretty certain would lead me to Old Chain of Rocks Bridge, though I'd have been more confident if there had actually been a sign. Sunlight was fading. I had to decide. So I turned right and headed down an unmarked two-lane road. After a few hundred yards I came to a one-lane bridge marked by a rather ominous sign: "Chouteau Island. Closed dusk to dawn."

You're thinking exactly what I should have been thinking. It's getting dark. I have no clue whether I'm on the correct road. I'm about to cross a rickety one-lane bridge to nowhere, and nowhere closes at dusk. Anyone in their right mind would have stopped. But I was determined, so up and over this creaky old bridge I went.

Chouteau Island looked deserted. The moment I exited the ancient bridge in fast-fading light I knew I'd made a mistake. In a few minutes it was going to be dark and I suddenly remembered the dangerous reputation of East St Louis. I didn't feel quite so determined any more.

Becky's phone call. "Where are you?" "I don't know." "I see you on the GPS." "I'll come back over the bridge." Whew! There's the trailer. We hugged in relief. We both knew I'd pushed it too far.

There's a fine line dividing perseverance from stupid risk, and I don't think the line's as clear as we imagine. It's easy in hindsight to distinguish stubbornness from tenacity, but at the decision point it's not always simple. God's not safe, and neither are God-inspired dreams. When you're following a dream you take some risks, and you do your best to find courage without recklessness.

However, I discovered one clear distinction. When it's getting dark and you're about to cross a dilapidated single-lane bridge with a sign proclaiming "Chouteau Island, closed dusk to dawn," you're probably about to cross from determined into stupid.

Amazing clarity can be gained simply from the perspective of a new day. The next morning Becky and I sat in bright sunshine at the base of the same single-lane bridge. A bit of research showed it was in fact the correct route, and it didn't look nearly so foreboding in the morning light. We unloaded the bike and arranged a meeting on the Missouri side of the river. I set off to finally see if Old Chain of Rocks Bridge was worthy of the effort and anticipation.

Chouteau Island turned out to be a redevelopment area. What looked like a scary wilderness the previous night was a reemerging neighborhood scattered with construction projects. I was still surprised by a lack of signs marking my approach to what was apparently a significant local tourist attraction. At least from the Illinois side nobody was going out of their way to publicize Old Chain of Rocks Bridge.

Finally I entered a small parking lot and discovered an almost secluded entrance to one of the narrowest bridges I'd ever seen. The sign told me this was once part of the legendary American highway known as Route 66. This thin ribbon of pavement, now open only to cycles and pedestrians, once constituted a portion of a major thoroughfare across the U.S.

Besides its limited width and being nearly a mile long, the Old Chain of Rocks Bridge is remarkable for two things. First, it's really steep, and I worked hard to crank up an incline designed to allow sufficient clearance for river traffic. The bridge also incorporates an unusual twenty-two-degree bend partway across.

The View From the Bridge

At the apex I had a great view of the river. I stopped and thought a bit about what I'd noticed about the river as I traveled and lived with it. The river's different from what you normally observe from the bridge.

I've lived in the Midwest for much of my life. I can't imagine how many times I've crossed the Mississippi River without paying much attention. At freeway speeds, the river's there one moment and gone the next. But when you travel along its length on a bike you have time to notice small stuff, subtle changes, things you don't see from the bridges. You realize the river isn't a constant ribbon of water. The river has a life of its own, and you can only perceive its nature by being with it for a while. Drive-by encounters won't do.

I think dreams look like that. It's difficult to grasp the scope of someone's dream when you zip past. You can't see details from a bridge at highway speed. When you live with a dream, it looks a lot different from how it appears on a quick fly-over. Maybe the idea that seems crazy from the freeway makes more sense when you travel with it awhile. Maybe we should be a bit slower to judge the worthiness of a dream when we cross it the first time.

The drive-by view explains partly why God-sized dreams shock people and make them nervous. Often those closest to you won't understand, at least initially, because they haven't lived with the dream like you have. Don't let their fear stop you. Maybe they'll get it after some time, or maybe you'll find others who do get it. Or maybe you won't. Dreams aren't about what other people think. Dreams are about what God thinks.

Becky and Monte waited for me partway across. We enjoyed splendid river views, shot some video, and chatted with a few tourists who recognized us from a news feature. The bridge restoration includes 1940s and '50s memorabilia recalling the heyday of the Route 66 era. It's fun to wonder about the adventurers who crossed the bridge and imagine the dreams people followed along its narrow corridor.

Old Chain of Rocks Bridge was a highlight, one of the scenes I'll always re-create when I picture the ride in my mind. It would have been easy to skip it and move on. We had miles to cover and places to go, and it was just an old abandoned bridge. I'm glad we took time to go back.

You need to stay focused when you're following a dream, but you need to focus on the right things. Old Chain of Rocks Bridge helped us remember this dream was never about covering miles. We're a culture of interstates and efficiency, but I saw the river more clearly sitting atop that pedestrian crossing than I ever did whizzing across a freeway span. That's the sort of perspective you need to understand and follow a river—or a dream.

You need to be careful not to run too fast when you're following a dream. A dream is an elusive thing that may not be right where you expect it. It's worth the time and effort to reach remarkable, out-of-the-way places. Sometimes that's where elusive things hang out.

Glamour

Some stretches of the river are positively glorious.

Bright sunlight shimmers across calm, impossibly blue water. Picturesque tugboats skillfully maneuver enormous barges through channels and locks. Lovely waterfront communities line the shore with resorts, trails, and parks. Refurbished downtown areas invite visitors to shop, dine, and relax in authentically restored historic settings. They're the postcard views featured on websites and chamber of commerce brochures.

But there are other stretches—oily backwaters; rusty abandoned barges; boarded-up buildings; and hard, weathered riverfront towns filled with hard, weathered people who wrestle a tough living from an unforgiving environment. Most tourists avoid these spots. They aren't quite what you imagine when you plan a trip along the river.

We saw this dichotomy in every river town. I concluded my ride in St. Louis on a wonderful eleven-mile riverfront trail linking Old Chain of Rocks Bridge to the iconic Gateway Arch, but in those miles I passed acres of dilapidated buildings and junky salvage yards. I crisscrossed through floodgates and across levees overlooking the difficult, less-than-picturesque work along the shore.

I understand the river only by experiencing all of it. Tourists frequent the restored communities filled with antique shops and souvenir stands, but those aren't the whole story. In some ways the tourist spots conceal a portion of reality like contrived movie sets. The river's more than snack shops and parks.

Same with a dream—it's not all the shining, glamorous adventure you imagine, the one portrayed in the movie. Just like the river, every dream includes hard, weathered stretches.

Parts of Rich's Ride were absolutely inspiring, glorious almost beyond description. The speaking events, the words of encouragement from the growing circle of support, the waves and shouts from drivers—those images capture what we imagined when we began. Everyone wants to hear those stories and see pictures of charming trails along calm, bright blue waters.

But the photo album pictures don't tell the entire story. Some parts were hard or boring or dangerous or downright discouraging. It's tempting to wish them away or pretend they didn't happen, but I can't and I shouldn't. I can't experience or explain the dream by hitting the tourist highlights.

Nearly anyone can do the easy parts. Cruising downhill in sunshine with a tailwind on a beautiful trail doesn't require much conditioning or develop much character. Those aren't the sorts of dreams to which God calls us.

You can see the river from the freeway in an air-conditioned car with cruise control. Easy, safe, and comfortable, but not the best way to gain a sense of the river's truth.

Parents, spouses, employees, and entrepreneurs all know

worthwhile journeys contain hard stretches. Those stretches must be traveled well. The river wouldn't be what it is without the tough parts. Same with the dream.

There's a saying among writers that nearly everyone likes having written but few are actually willing to commit to the difficult process of writing. Perhaps there's an analogous question about a dream and your commitment to it. Would you really want to start a business, with all the work and risk and grimy details? Or do you simply want the result—the nice, clean feeling of having started a business? Do you really want to serve, or are you willing to endure serving to get to the feeling of having served?

Having done is the glamorous part where you get the attention and praise. It's where everyone pats you on the back and tells you how great you are while you pretend to be overwhelmed by undeserved accolades. Nobody's immune from being tempted by the glory of *having done*, but it's the wrong reason to follow a dream.

Whatever the dream, do you seek the warm-fuzzy glow of *having done* it? Are you after some version of an "attaboy"? Will you be secretly disappointed if nobody notices? Is there some spot deep inside where you don't want to go, where you imagine God will be just a little bit impressed once you've done this thing?

There's nothing wrong with enjoying the good feelings from having done something worthwhile. I absolutely like having done Rich's Ride, but that's not why I did it. Having done it earns me only the opportunity to learn from our efforts, leverage them, and continue toward God's next task for Becky and me.

God doesn't call us to be people who've done things so we can sit on the front porch in a rocking chair and recount the glory days. He invites us to do big things, to dream big dreams and follow them. But be prepared, because following God-sized dreams takes you through some stretches that aren't roses and sunshine.

Some stretches of the river are positively glorious. Some aren't. I wonder if the trip might ultimately be defined by how we travel the less-glamorous stretches.

Stop planning. Start preparing.

week 1

1 Steve & Mark dip handcycle wheels in Mississippi River's source
2 Rich, Monte, & Paul Bunyan
3 Becky, Steve, Rich, & Monte before blast-off
4 Elk River Day—kids in the park
5 Evening of Elk River Day
6 TV interview in Bemidji

3
4
5
6
GULF OF
MEXICO
rich's ride
Together
HOPE
CONVOY OF HOPE

week 2

1 Tour of dreams stops at Field of Dre
2 An amazing cake decorated by my
3 Rich & Monte at Field of Dreams
4 Hills of Western Wisconsin
5 TV in La Crosse
6 Luther HS in La Crosse
7 Kids loved Monte & the bike

4
5
6

week 3

1. *Illinois has hills!*
2. *Youth night in Rock Island*
3. *Glenn, Rich, & Chief Keokuk at the top of Anschutz Hill*

week 4

1 *Jon Swanson, Rich, & Monte*
2 *St Louis Arch—halfway!*
3 *Chain of Rocks Bridge*

week 5

1. *Rich, Bruce, and Chi Oemga students in Carbondale*
2. *Cape Girardeau Christian School*
3. *Youth Night in Carbondale*
4. *Carbondale Christian HS*
5. *Carbondale soccer players*
6. *Cape Girardeau Elementary kids*

5

6

week 6

1 Left to right, "Cousin Dudley" & Melissa Boyd and Nena & Rob Lyons present a donation from National Bankers Trust in Memphis

week 7

1 Bike jersey
2 Galloway Church in Jackson, Ms
3 The star of the show
4 Rolling Fork hospital welcoming committee
5 Homeless in Jackson
6 Our Jackson hosts: Moise, cousin Rachel, and Sara
7 Rich & niece Sara
8 Youth group in Jackson

5
6
7
8

week 8

1. *Becky, Rich, & Monte: We made it!*
2. *Dick DeCook & his cool banner*
3. *Phong tries out the bike*
4. *Part of the HEC group in New Orleans*
5. *Convoy of Hope warehouse*
6. *CELEBRATION!*

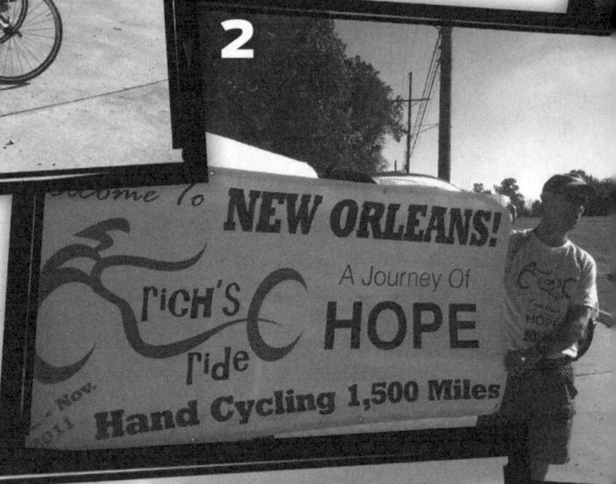

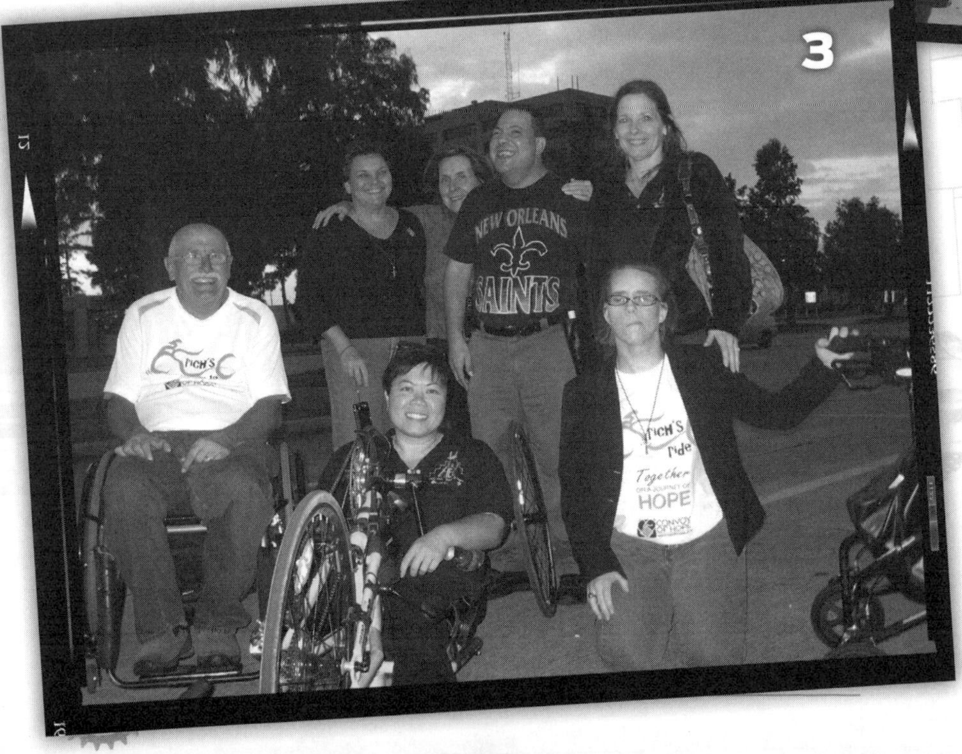

2

3

4
5
6

15 detours

Blessed are the flexible, for they shall not be broken.

At the beginning of our journey as we prepared to leave Fort Collins, Mark Orphan offered these parting words: "Blessed are the flexible, for they shall not be broken." Mark's personal beatitude proved remarkably prophetic because dreams, like rivers, don't travel directly from point A to point B.

Most folks familiar with American geography generally think of the Mississippi River as a strip of water flowing south from Lake Itasca to New Orleans. Few people realize its initial route heads north; in short stretches it actually flows east or west; and at one point north of Wabasha, Minnesota, the river is so wide it's actually called Lake Pepin.

You can't follow the river's exact course because in most places no road or trail directly parallels the shore. So while Rich's Ride was billed as a ride along the Mississippi River, we actually followed the general route of the river, crossed it a lot, and rode beside it a few times. Mostly we sort of meandered in the same general direction as the river.

That's how a dream works. You know where you're trying to go and you get a general notion of the route, but you figure out details as you go because life's rarely ideal or predictable. Dreamers tend to chafe against this uncomfortable reality. Any deviation from the plan is perceived as an undesirable delay.

As a teacher I watched kids become frustrated with school because it seemed to keep them from getting on with their dreams. Sometimes that's true, but often a class or a degree that seems like a detour actually leads to the opportunity we're seeking. We frequently don't know what we're looking for until we find it, so an apparent diversion might take us precisely where we ought to go or at least give us time to learn and grow and figure out the true essentials. "Wants" and "needs" aren't always located on the same path.

Some detours actually delay or knock us off course for a season. Illness, financial setbacks, family issues—all sorts of detours pop up where we don't expect them. But they're only detours and they're temporary. Just like the river, the dream's still there, even when we can't see it. So we cling to hope, because hope assures we'll eventually discover a path back to the river. We have to believe and trust and keep moving because one's thing's certain—sitting still and complaining won't get us back to our dream.

And then there are moments when we call a deliberate "timeout" and intentionally veer away from the dream's intended course. Charging full-speed in single-minded pursuit might seem like the quickest path to success, but wise dream-followers know better. Apparent diversions often become essential experiences and contribute to long-term success when we're following a God-sized dream.

On Rich's Ride, Carbondale, Illinois, wasn't a place. It was an event.

On a map, Carbondale looks like a city about forty miles east of the river. About three weeks into the ride Becky received an invitation to visit Carbondale. Bruce Payne, who worked with Dale Crall, a close friend of Dick Foth (we felt confused, too), offered to host us and arrange speaking opportunities. Bruce's excitement and enthusiasm for our mission made it easy to choose one of those intentional detours.

Have you ever felt like you were meeting an old friend for the first time? That's how it felt as we met Bruce in the parking lot at Heartland Christian Center for our first Carbondale speaking engagement. I enjoyed the presentation and discussion, but we really appreciated the easy familiarity of getting to know Bruce. He clearly "got" what we were doing and shared our passion. We felt an easy reassurance. Carbondale would be a productive course change.

Bruce told us we'd meet later with players from the Carbondale Community High School soccer team. I wasn't exactly clear about setting or context, but by this point I figured I could tell the story to just about any group. I was a bit intimidated when I arrived and discovered both boys' and girls' teams were present, but I'd been invited to give essentially a pregame talk for the boys before their final home game of the season. It was senior night and a rivalry game with playoff implications. As high school games go, this was a big night for these kids and Coach Jeff Hansen.

We met a lot of remarkable people doing remarkable things along Rich's Ride. Actually, that's probably not right. We really met a lot of pretty ordinary people doing remarkable things. Mostly they didn't think much about being special. They were just doing whatever they were doing, where they were, with what they had.

Jeff was a great example of an ordinary guy doing something remarkable. If you watched casually you might see just a coach and some players. But nearly every kid went out of the way to greet him, and he always responded in a genuine, personal manner. You couldn't distinguish star players. He was busy getting us set up, as well as thinking about and preparing for an important evening, but no kid walked away feeling brushed off. This guy cared about every kid. I'm sure he had a lot on his mind, but I never felt rushed or in the way. He truly wanted his kids to hear about hope and overcoming adversity and something bigger than a game.

Patents told us he built an amazing program in a couple of years. I don't think it's because he was an exceptional coach. I think he made a difference in individual lives, one kid at a time, every day. When we talked, he was clear about giving credit to others and telling us he wasn't doing anything special. And he's right. He was just doing what all of us can do. He had the audacity to believe he could touch hearts and change lives, right where he was.

Ever think you don't really matter and you can't change the world? I do, and I'll bet you do, and we're wrong. You don't have to be rich or famous or powerful. The so-called world-changers don't really change individual lives. You and I have that power, every day, right where we are. The coach was changing the world. Each of us gets the same opportunity.

We see people like him every day. We're surrounded by them, but too often we don't notice their remarkable acts. One of the incredible blessings of Rich's Ride was the opportunity to escape my familiar environment and be a bit more aware of the everyday kindness and generosity I so frequently take for granted.

Speaking to a team, especially in a pregame setting, was a new experience. I wanted to say something meaningful without overwhelming them, so I began with a simple question: "When a game ends, how do you know if you won?"

Eyes migrated toward the scoreboard. A few pointed. Pretty obvious—the team with the most goals wins the game.

"And who knows which team won?"

They hesitated before someone replied, "Well, everyone. You just have to read the score."

"Of course. Everyone knows which team won. Now here's a tougher one.

"Who controls the outcome of the game?"

Immediately one player shouted, "We do!"

I waited and let his idea sink in for a second. "Really? You're in complete control of the outcome?"

Of course they knew better. All good athletes acknowledge issues beyond their command and strive to focus on what they can control. We listed a few examples of factors that might influence a game's outcome: weather or field conditions, opponents' skill and resolve, good or bad bounces, officials' decisions. It's just a fact: Sometimes the best or most determined team doesn't win the game.

Then I changed course. "How do you know if you're a winner?" Curiously, no one looked at the scoreboard. "And who knows if you're a winner?"

It was quiet, so I waited. Finally a young lady said quietly, "I do."

I smiled. "That one's harder, huh? The scoreboard tells who won, but only you, in here," I put my hand on my chest, "can know if you're a winner."

At this point I felt uncertain about how much deeper to go. I know how coaches feel about cluttering their players' minds before a game. But I sensed Jeff would be okay with talking about something bigger than game strategy, and it was sort of too late to stop anyway.

I adapted my notion of "being a winner" from the television show *Friday Night Lights*, which followed a coach and his team through the craziness of Texas high school football. The team adopted a unique rallying cry focused on the difference between "winning" and "being a winner."

"Clear eyes. Full hearts. Can't lose."

I explained my interpretation to the players.

"Have you ever tried to look in a mirror after you 'got away' with something? Maybe you broke a rule or lied and didn't get caught, or took a shortcut in a practice drill and the coach didn't notice. Maybe you know you didn't give your best, but somehow it worked out okay and everyone's patting you on the back and telling you how great you are. And maybe you smile and accept the praise, but when you look in the mirror it doesn't feel so good.

"Do you know the feeling I'm talking about—when it's hard to look at the person in the mirror because he or she knows you're hiding something?" A few heads nodded slowly. "We've all had that feeling. We all know what it's like to think we got away with less than our best, only to endure the crummy feeling of being afraid to face the person in the mirror. It's like you almost can't look, or you want to hide."

So far this wasn't exactly a rousing pregame speech.

"Now turn it around. Think about what it's like to look in the mirror when you know you did the right thing, when you know you did your best. Maybe you're disappointed because you didn't get the results you wanted; maybe nobody else noticed. Is it different to look in the mirror?"

Heads nodded.

"That's 'clear eyes.' When you can gaze at the man or woman in the mirror and not be afraid or look away, when you know he or she knows you did it right, you're a winner. Winners live with clear eyes.

"Now think about the people who care about you: family, friends, teammates. Think about what it's like when you know you let them down because you didn't keep commitments or do your best. Maybe it's gossip, or you didn't hustle on a play, or you weren't where you said you'd be. And let's say they didn't notice.

"What's it like to face them around the dinner table or in the locker room? They don't know, or you don't think they know. Where does that hurt?"

I pointed to my head. No. Then I put hand on heart. Heads nodded.

"Now think about the locker room when everyone gave it everything they had. Think about how it feels when you know you kept your promise when it was hard, when you made a tough play for a teammate." They were smiling. "Where does that feel good?"

Several kids pointed to their chests.

"That's a 'full heart.' A full heart is about love. It means you're connected to your friends, family, or teammates. It means you're willing to sacrifice for their benefit, for some goal bigger than self-interest. When you have a full heart, you know it's not about you. You've got your buddies' backs, and they've got yours.

"When you play and live like that, you're filling your heart with love. That's what winners do. Winners live with full hearts.

"If you play—if you live—with clear eyes and a full heart, you're a winner.

"You may not always win. You don't control the scoreboard. But you can always—always—be a winner!

"And here's the really amazing thing. We're wired to live with clear eyes and a full heart. We're created to be winners. And when we operate like winners, we give ourselves the best chance to win.

"There's no guarantee. We all know losers sometimes win in the short term. But being a winner, living with clear eyes and a full heart, gives us the best shot at winning in the long run. And that's what matters."

One-shot inspirational speeches probably aren't the best way to create lasting impact. I don't know how much those kids really assimilated my message. They smiled and nodded, but I'm sure their minds bounced in a thousand different directions and I was just some old guy on a crazy bike ride. I hope something clicked with one or two kids and maybe added to stuff they'd heard before.

I do know the team lost their game, 2-1. Thus endeth my budding career as pregame speaker guaranteed to produce wins.

I thought a lot about clear eyes/full hearts during the ride. Becky and I made mistakes, missed opportunities, and discovered better ways of doing many things. I suppose the scoreboard might argue whether we won or lost. Like the game, win or lose lies mostly beyond our control.

But when you take a God-sized risk and follow a dream, you hit the pillow each night with clear eyes and a full heart.

Youth Night

The event we called "Carbondale" would have been a success if it had ended right there, but Bruce was just getting started. The next morning we spoke to a wonderful group of high school students. Then we spent the afternoon with a group of "nontraditional" students, members of Chi Omega at a local community college. They told incredible stories of following Jesus and pursuing educational goals despite financial, cultural, and social obstacles. Their journeys reminded me of the truly smooth road I'm blessed to ride.

After dinner we met in the parking lot of an old warehouse. Bruce and Becky unloaded the trailer while I watched the familiar commotion of teenagers entering the rundown building. Each time the door opened, music blared into the night as kids converged on an unconventional youth group.

Bruce told us these young people arrived mostly by bus from low-income housing projects. We'd somehow overlooked those areas during two days in what seemed like a stereotypical middle class university town. I guess we tend to see only what's familiar, or perhaps what we look for. In this cavernous space filled with worship music and adolescent energy, the need couldn't be missed.

While I waited to speak I listened to the director of the youth center. He told me nearly every one of the hundred kids in the room would go home to some form of abuse or neglect—if they had a home at all. Several were homeless, living either in cars or as "couch surfers." As I watched their worship time I wondered what I could possibly say to impact their circumstances. Then I remembered they were there to worship. It wasn't me they leaned upon. They'd come to connect with the One who could change hearts and alter the course of lives.

So I talked and tried to be vulnerable. I hope I said something meaningful. They laughed, seemed impressed with the story of the ride, and hung out afterwards to talk and check out the bike. I was acutely aware their world wasn't going to be repaired by me or my words. I couldn't scratch the surface of their needs. I could simply do the task Jesus placed before me on a specific night, and trust Him for the rest. That's what those kids were doing. In the end, it's what all of us can do.

You can leave that kind of experience in one of two ways. You might be sad, angry, or depressed about hungry, abused kids who don't seem to have a fair shake. You can feel impotent in the face of so much unmet need in the midst of abundance.

Or you can choose to be grateful. Grateful for youth pastors and volunteers who don't ignore these kids, for donors who support the work of critically important ministries, for kids whose hearts are open to Jesus even in tough circumstances. You can be grateful for the opportunity to share an evening with these folks, to contribute in your own small way. You can be grateful for the ability to follow a dream and encourage others to follow theirs.

Choosing gratitude doesn't mean ignoring the needs. It means acknowledging you can't solve them, either, but you can resolve to continue to do what you can, where you are, with what you have.

Clear eyes. Full heart.

Can't lose.

Dreams are like rivers. They don't travel directly from point A to point B.

I can't imagine Rich's Ride without the apparent detour that turned out to be the blessing of Carbondale and our wonderful friend Bruce. We would still have reached the end, but the experience would have been less rich and diverse.

You can't look at the roads away from the river as wasted time, something to simply endure. Those miles offer their own beauty and their own lessons. Whether the diversion's intended or not, it's part of following the dream. The choice is whether to resent or embrace.

Embracing leaves you with clear eyes and a full heart.

Blessed are the flexible, for they shall not be broken.

notes

16 lessons from cape G

It's about the journey and the destination.

Do you not know that in a race all the runners run, but only one gets the prize? Run in such a way as to get the prize. (1 Corinthians 9:24)

Which matters more—journey or destination? We're easily drawn into false dilemmas, artificially concocted choices designed to frame our thinking in "one or the other" terms. But in most circumstances I don't really have to select paper or plastic. Usually there's a third, superior option.

False dilemmas are just what the term implies—they're false. They fabricate an artificial line and frame discussion in terms of choosing the proper side of the line. Often it's the wrong debate. Is this the right line? Does a line even exist?

Which of my 255 TV channels should I watch? It's a false dilemma. Maybe I should read a book or play with the dog. Which is more important—journey or destination? Perhaps there's another option.

Before the ride began Becky and I spent hours setting goals, planning, figuring out where we wanted to go and what we wished to accomplish. It's all destination material, and it matters. Paul told us, "Run in such a way as to get the prize." The prize, the result, the destination—all are important.

The problem, of course, is too frequently we fix our gaze exclusively on the finish line. Getting there becomes our sole thought; but the Bible says, "Run in such a way as to get the prize." Apparently there's a proper means for reaching the finish line. How we travel matters.

Should I focus on the prize or how I pursue it? Rich's Ride taught us it's really about both.

Before we decided to follow the Mississippi River's path, I'd never heard of Cape Girardeau, Missouri. When we announced our route, several friends and supporters provided numerous Cape G contacts who expressed interest in arranging speaking opportunities. We planned a busy weekend, and this unfamiliar city promised to become a focal point for Rich's Ride.

For many unrelated reasons that really weren't anyone's fault, most of those events didn't materialize. We met with a great group of kids and enjoyed a wonderful conversation with U.S. Congresswoman Jo Ann Emerson. Otherwise, our much-anticipated weekend in Cape Girardeau passed quietly.

It would have been easy to be disappointed, to perceive unfulfilled plans as failure or wasted opportunity. But dreams aren't efficient, and adventures aren't preplanned tours. Becky kept reminding me God would bring us together with the right people and opportunities. Even though the weekend wasn't exactly what we intended, the days still contained important lessons.

Because things worked out differently from what we planned, my riding schedule around Cape G was a bit unusual. I actually rode to the city twice from different directions. On Thursday I cranked from Carbondale on the Illinois side. When a Friday event didn't come together, I backtracked and approached on the Missouri side. Similar distance, same destination, but two rides couldn't have been more different.

Thursday's route followed an Illinois highway that might have been anywhere in rural America. Roads past cornfields provided smooth, wide shoulders and relatively safe riding despite constant traffic. I hardly shifted gears to negotiate infrequent, long, gradual hills.

Friday brought country roads with little traffic, nonexistent bike lanes, and nonstop, incredibly steep hills. I either crawled up difficult inclines or coasted perhaps a bit too quickly downhill.

Thursday's highway ride was noisy, not especially scenic, and fairly easy. It was all about rhythm and consistent cranking.

Friday permitted absolutely no rhythm, but featured quiet roads, beautiful farms, and constantly alternating uphill struggles and downhill thrills. Two days afforded two distinctly different rides along dissimilar routes, but both concluded in the same city after covering similar distances in the same time and average speed.

One might ask if the rides were similar or completely different. Depends on whether you're focused on process or result. Vastly divergent experiences produced almost duplicate results.

A dream is the God-inspired desire
to share your unique gifts and passions
to serve others and change the world.

"Change the world" is the destination. The result matters. The kind of change you create is important.

But life happens on the road. "Share" and "serve" are the process, the experience, the way you run the race. Getting there is great, but how you get there matters, too. Getting there the right way, enjoying and learning from the journey, makes getting there worth the effort.

Traveling well matters, and a big part of traveling well is avoiding silly comparisons. These two rides provided different experiences, each with its own challenges and joys. The trick is to appreciate each day for itself and its gifts rather than wasting precious attention comparing the rides. Neither was better or worse than the other. Each, in its own unique way, provided all we needed and taught an important lesson.

Our weekend in Cape Girardeau marked the beginning of Week 6. As I took some time to think back and reflect, I noticed another lesson from the first five weeks of Rich's Ride.

My initial idea was to ride two hundred miles during each of the first seven weeks, leaving only one hundred miles during the final week to reach the fifteen-hundred-mile goal. I also planned to ride a little extra distance during the first few weeks when I was fresh to create a cushion in case I faded toward the end.

We started each week with a plan to exceed two hundred miles, and something always got in the way. Weather, difficult terrain, equipment issues, last-minute speaking opportunities—something always kept us from creating that small bit of insurance against future problems. But we were always able to maintain the original schedule. We didn't get ahead, but we didn't fall behind. We were able to do just enough.

This pattern reminds me of the manna God provided to the Israelites in the desert. They couldn't collect extra; they got what they needed for the day and learned to trust God's provision for the next day.

Maybe it's one more lesson from Rich's Ride. I'm slowly learning to allow each day to take care of itself, trusting the next day for its own issues and rewards. God provides what I need each day. I need to learn how to be content with just enough.

It's about the journey and the destination.

17 dog evangelism

You don't really know how strong you are until being strong is your only choice.

I trained hard for this ride. I thought I was about as prepared as possible, but it didn't take long to understand that training isn't the same as the real thing. I learned something important about preparing in life.

When I ride at home, preparing and training, it's too easy to cut a ride short when I get tired. I can avoid the really tough hills when I'm struggling and adjust my route depending on the wind. If the weather's too bad or I'm really tired I can easily skip a day.

Those options disappeared on Rich's Ride. I needed to progress regardless of weather, wind, or terrain. I had to face whatever appeared before me. I couldn't choose to ride a different direction or skip the hilly sections. Easy or hard, sun or clouds, warm or cold didn't matter. My only choice was ride or don't ride, and either choice had real consequences.

I discovered I'm a better rider than I realized. I've handcycled for more than ten years, cranked more than twenty-five thousand miles around my hometown. I thought I knew my limits, but those "limits" turned out to be largely self-imposed. I can ride faster and farther and tackle tougher terrain than I imagined. I discovered my true capabilities only when I had no other choice.

I think about how I often respond to everyday circumstances. I believe I'm living a life of integrity, but I frequently choose the easy path, avoiding tough decisions and unpleasant conflict whenever possible. How well am I preparing or training for the inevitable adversity I'll encounter at some point?

We claim to trust God's provision, but most of us live with a built-in safety net offering easy escape when things get too tough. We don't approach our actual capabilities because we don't need to. As long as the net's there, we never quite know how we'd respond if it suddenly disappeared.

Dream-following isn't comfortable. God-sized dreams don't include safety nets.

Maybe I tackled something crazy-big like this ride because it's one way to see what I can do when I don't have an easy escape and quitting has readily apparent consequences. Perhaps it's good to purposely step beyond our "easy zone" just to determine our true capabilities.

Dream-following isn't thrill-seeking for its own sake, because dreams aren't about the dreamer. Dreams invite us to pursue a bigger purpose than we can imagine on our own. Following a dream means leaning on God for what seems impossible. You follow a dream with hope that allows you to believe despite the evidence, and then watch the evidence change.

In hindsight it's easy to imagine a point at which completing the ride became a foregone conclusion. In reality the ride probably became more difficult as we progressed. Each day presented unexpected obstacles. Even as I became stronger, other challenges made reaching the finish line far from inevitable. In other circumstances I'm certain I would have taken additional rest days to allow sore old muscles, a tired mind, and a worn-out backside to recuperate.

I exceeded what I believed possible. Maybe you can only do that when doing more is your only choice.

In Sikeston, Missouri, we encountered a tourist landmark disguised as a local restaurant. Lambert's Cafe created its reputation based on "Throwed Rolls." Seriously. When you want another roll you raise your hand and a guy tosses it across the room. The food's wonderful, manager and staff made sure we left with great memories, and the "throwed rolls" were actually quite tasty. We had a great time.

Customers demonstrated varying degrees of proficiency as roll catchers, so the remnants of tossed food made Lambert's a highlight for Monte. He's normally quite disciplined in restaurants, but this particular floor offered constant temptation. He became a secondary source of entertainment to those seated around us as he tried not so subtly to clean his portion of the floor without being noticed. As an eighty-pound bundle of fur, Monte rarely goes unnoticed.

Lambert's also generated two examples of dog evangelism. Becky and I understand from experience that Monte's loving eyes and floppy ears often reach out to people and breach walls impervious to our words. It's not proper service dog etiquette, but we're convinced part of his service is drawing people into our circle with his gentle spirit. We simply sit back and watch him work his unique magic.

A young girl at the next table asked if she could pet Monte. As soon as she extended a hand, Monte rested his blocky head in her lap while she stroked and scratched and almost cuddled with him. Everyone around us smiled, and Becky began a conversation with the little girl's mom.

This was the first day of their new life. They'd left a bad situation and moved to a new city, a new job, and a fresh start. Mom talked about her mixture of anticipation and fear and her daughter's anxiety about an unfamiliar school and finding new friends. As we chatted, Monte continued to tilt his head this way and that to get a scratch in every conceivable spot. We talked about Mom's concern for her daughter and about the ride, about hope and possibilities and God's faithfulness, while Monte comforted a child in a manner beyond human understanding.

After they left, Becky and I just looked at each other in wonder. We talked a little about the incredible ways God works when we manage to stay out of His way. We knew a girl and her mom felt just a bit more peaceful and hopeful, and the whole process had very little to do with us. Monte, of course, moved on, because he's always in the present moment. He'd done his part and went back to searching for crumbs.

A few minutes later a woman approached and asked if she could join us. She had observed our earlier exchange and wanted to talk about what she saw. Of course she complimented Monte, who happily accepted her praise and scratches as though nobody ever paid any attention to him. She wanted to know about our bike jerseys and the ride. She stayed a few minutes, then asked us to wait while she retrieved her purse. She wrote an extremely generous donation check to Convoy of Hope. "Please take this in honor of Monte and his kind, tender spirit. He's a gift from God."

Publicity and fund-raising aren't difficult. You need only an eighty-pound people magnet with a gentle, loving face and floppy ears.

Later that evening the Rich's Ride Facebook page included two comments—one from the mother of a little girl and one from a new donor/supporter. Both expressed gratitude for the opportunity to meet Monte. I think they may have mentioned Becky and me as well, but the comments left no doubt about which member of our team made the real impact.

Dog evangelism.

Crazy Rain

The next morning brought the worst weather of the entire trip. We awoke to low-forties temperatures, wind, rain, and sleet. At home, such conditions are a prescription for another cup of coffee and no riding.

Becky advised waiting, but I was determined to proceed. I wrapped myself in layers, donned rain gear, and started cranking. It wasn't the most pleasant ride I've experienced, but the day reminded me of an important principle: Dream-following tests and expands your limits because it's more about character than comfort.

Character is a long-term issue, often developed and tested in uncomfortable settings. I could easily have chosen the short-term comfort of a hotel lobby. Everyone who watched me get ready thought I was nuts for venturing into such miserable conditions, and perhaps they were right.

But a difficult ride took me past the thousand-mile mark. I rode faster than any previous day of the entire journey. I proved to myself I could continue to follow my dream in the face of difficult circumstances. Those things matter to me. They were worth sacrificing a few hours of short-term comfort.

A flat tire helped us decide to cut the ride a bit short. I didn't want Becky to help change wheels while we both got soaked and chilled, so we called it a day.

Some might wonder why I purposely surrendered certain comfort for a thirty-four-mile bike ride in crummy conditions. I'm sure passing drivers questioned my sanity. Riding in cold rain has costs, but from my perspective the cost of not riding was too high. I'm glad I didn't exchange a difficult, rewarding, satisfying ride for a small bit of short-term comfort.

I wonder how often we pass by remarkable experiences to avoid temporary discomfort. I wonder if we understand the price we pay for the safety net. I think God invites us to reject "comfort at any cost."

You don't really know how strong you are until being strong is your only choice.

notes

18 heartsong

It's not about me. (Repeat as necessary.)

Let your light shine before others, that they may see your good deeds and glorify your Father in heaven. (Matthew 5:16)

The right question usually matters more than the right answer.

I believe in the guidance and wisdom of questions. Ever notice how some questions keep appearing? Maybe you ignore them or you think you've answered them, but they keep popping up in all sorts of different places. When a question comes at you from different sources and angles, maybe it's trying to tell you something important.

As a teacher I learned to be more comfortable and satisfied with hard questions than easy answers. Asking good questions mattered more than providing right answers. I learned to be guided by students' questions. Questions reveal what's really being processed, what really matters to listeners. Answers lead to endings and closed doors. Questions provide beginnings because they indicate which doors might need to be opened. Answers tell me what someone knows. Questions tell me what they want, or need, to know. Questions provide opportunities to serve.

The best response to a question depends on context and relationship. Great communicators know when to provide an answer or ask another, deeper question. Secure communicators know it's okay to say, "I don't know." And when a difficult, life-changing, soul-stirring question springs from the heart, compassionate communicators know when to say, "Let's figure it out together."

I think that's often God's response to my questions. I want a quick answer, but He knows I need a companion and guide as I search. "Wants" and "needs" aren't always located on the same path.

From the very beginning of Rich's Ride two questions became part of the project's DNA. Initially I thought I knew the answers. At nearly every speaking event, some form of these questions arose, and I realized my preconceived responses began to evolve. At some point I knew discovering what I could about them was an integral part of the project.

What's next? From first week to final day, people wanted to know where this dream led once we reached New Orleans. They implicitly assumed this particular project was part of something bigger. I'll explore this notion in the final chapter.

Why? It's a powerful question. Initially I thought it meant "What made you do something this crazy?" Eventually I understood its true meaning: "How can I find the courage to follow my own dream?"

Cousin Dudley

This kind of enterprise develops its own language. Sometime during Week 3, Becky started telling me about Cousin Dudley in Memphis. Dick Foth had connected her with his cousin Dudley Boyd, CEO of National Bankers Trust. Dudley happily agreed to host us for the weekend, though truthfully his wife, Melissa, did the hard work of making arrangements for our time in Memphis. Nevertheless, just as Paul Bunyan was a trail and Carbondale was an event, Memphis was associated with Cousin Dudley in the vernacular of Rich's Ride.

Melissa and Dudley exceeded any reasonable definition of hospitality. First they arranged a prepaid weekend at the historic (and luxurious) Peabody Hotel. If you've never heard of the Peabody Ducks, check them out on YouTube. Aside from worrying how Monte might react to ducks waddling through the hotel lobby, we thoroughly enjoyed being pampered after six weeks on the road. We met our new friends and their business partners for a wonderful meal, and I managed a relaxing ride along a beautiful urban bike corridor.

They also invited us to share our story at their church. Among the many wonderful churches we visited along the ride, this one had perhaps the most memorable, descriptive name: Heartsong Church. It's situated in a quiet, secluded setting, and I recall an especially peaceful vibe about the morning, the people, and the idea of discovering and sharing a "heart song."

Cousin Dudley's church provided a relaxed atmosphere for conversations. Maybe that's why a number of folks took time to inquire about the reasons behind the ride: "Why are you doing it?" "What led you to such a big commitment?" "What is the real mission?"

Maybe Heartsong was the place to finally examine why we were doing this thing called Rich's Ride. I don't think we always understand why we decide to follow a particular dream until we've traveled some of the road. Perhaps this was the appointed moment to understand the true inspiration behind this expedition.

Rich's Ride wasn't inspired by the activities that consumed so much of our effort. It was never primarily about fund-raising. By the time we reached Memphis we knew we'd end up collecting a substantial sum, and we celebrate the generosity that ultimately provided nearly $60,000 for starving children. But as a fund-raiser our project was pretty inefficient. There are much faster, easier, and more scalable ways to address the financial side of poverty issues.

Dream-following isn't especially efficient. Dreams don't operate like factories with assembly lines and repeatable, quality-controlled processes. Dream-following is an adventure, a figure-it-out-as-you-go operation. It can't be all nailed down and buttoned up before you begin. Wandering and backtracking and restarting are all innate parts of following dreams. Dreams inspire. Assembly lines maximize efficiency, but they don't stir the soul.

Supporting the incredible efforts of Convoy of Hope to feed hungry kids was clearly an integral part of what happened during Rich's Ride. But the "why" was something deeper.

It certainly wasn't about attracting attention. In fact, you might evaluate your commitment to a dream by asking honestly if you'd still do it even if nobody noticed. I think you might be in trouble if you're following a God-sized dream for attention or personal glory.

Honestly, I struggled with this issue because we worked hard to publicize the ride. We issued press releases, did media spots, sought speaking gigs, posted blog updates, and tried to stay current with social media. By many measures we attracted quite a bit of attention and a modest following. Why did we try so hard to get noticed if we weren't trying to get noticed? I wondered if I was playing around at some sort of fake humility, claiming I didn't want attention while desperately seeking it.

Obviously it made little sense to keep the ride a secret. We couldn't expect to collect donations and raise awareness for Convoy of Hope by hiding in a corner. We couldn't share an important story of hope and God's faithfulness if no one knew about it. But I still felt uncomfortable about being the focus of all the attention, the public face of the efforts of so many others. Even the title, Rich's Ride, felt awkward because it somehow conveyed a sense of "Look at me!"

You are the light of the world. A town built on a hill cannot be hidden. Neither do people light a lamp and put it under a bowl. Instead they put it on its stand, and it gives light to everyone in the house. In the same way, let your light shine before others, that they may see your good deeds and glorify your Father in heaven. (Matthew 5:14–16)

I tend to lose sight of those last five words: "glorify your Father in heaven." Rich's Ride taught me many important lessons, but perhaps the most essential is *it's not about me*. In fact, if I really was doing this crazy journey for right reasons it would be arrogant and irresponsible not to proclaim it. The lamp isn't the center of attention. We display the lighted lamp because it focuses attention on God.

I truly believe this dream was a God-inspired desire. I don't blame God lightly for my ideas and thoughts, but I'm confident He placed the seed of Rich's Ride in my heart and nurtured it for a decade. I believe He provided the right people at the right time to help me see the true potential and power of this dream. And since I believe this effort was God-inspired, why in the world would I try to hide it?

So I speak and write about Rich's Ride whenever I can. I believe the story of hope and God's faithfulness can help others. I'm writing this book, and I hope people buy it and read it and share it. I'll do my best to promote it, but the publicity isn't about getting noticed. It's not about me!

We did fund-raising and publicity. We sought speaking opportunities. We sold books and tried to form lasting relationships that might lead to future opportunities. And I'm claiming, I hope honestly, that the ride really wasn't about the major activities in which we engaged. The whole point of creating light was to illuminate God's glory.

Earlier I mentioned a false humility that seeks attention while claiming to not want it. The other end of the spectrum might be false superiority, a sense that I'm above promoting worthwhile endeavors. But if I believe God's involved, if I'm doing something that might touch a heart or help someone feel a bit less isolated, who am I to not tell others what's happening?

Perhaps Cousin Dudley's Heartsong Church was the perfect place to examine "Why am I doing this?" because Rich's Ride was, in many respects, a "heart song." This entire project began because I thought I wanted to take a bike ride to fulfill an item on a bucket list. It became a continuation of the story of hope from *Relentless Grace* and a way of saying thank you for the incredible good God brought from the tragedy of my injury. It was an attempt to live a story of hope and demonstrate that life is determined by availability and possibility, not by disability.

It was all of those, but really it was a God-inspired desire to share my unique gifts and passions to serve others and change the world. The handcycle, the ride, the fund-raising, the speaking and writing—those were all details. Those were the tools God provided.

In many ways it would have been simpler to say no to this dream. *No* was the easy answer, the one with a thousand reasons to support it. *No* didn't even require a reason as long as I didn't tell anyone else. Nobody would have thought less of me for turning away from such a difficult, irrational undertaking.

No was the safe, sensible answer. *No* would have alleviated the fears and maintained my comfortable status quo. *No* would have avoided a lot of effort and uncertainty. By most objective standards, *No* was the right answer to this dream. It was my answer for a long time.

At some point potential regret and missed opportunity outweighed fear. Security mattered less than possibility, and reasons mattered less than the sense in my heart. Even when the obvious right answer was no, my answer became yes.

I believe my yes came from God. I believe that's His nature, His character. He's the God of an amazing future, not a status quo past. He's the God of big dreams and incredible possibilities. He invites us to lean on Him and step out boldly to claim His promises. I believe He inspires each of us to use our unique gifts and passions in service.

In the end, I had to say yes because this dream wasn't about me. Rich's Ride was a God-sized dream. It seems too easy to claim that its purpose was to glorify God, but that's exactly what it was about. The rest is details.

I believe in the guidance and wisdom of questions. It took a while, but Heartsong helped me understand "why?"

It's not about me. (Repeat as necessary.)

19 the middle of nowhere

Stepping out in faith sometimes takes you to uncomfortable places in the middle of nowhere.

Many days of Rich's Ride were pretty ordinary. Dreams, even God-sized endeavors, are like that. A lot of it is just a daily grind, doing the ordinary stuff to get from one place to the next. You frequently find yourself in the middle of nowhere, sometimes in a city and sometimes on a deserted country road. The middle of nowhere is a place where you don't recognize any landmarks and don't have any points of reference. You just keep going, not because it's glamorous or because you see any immediate result but because you believe there's somewhere you're supposed to go or because you're just having fun going.

You don't take these days for granted because they're really what the project's about. They're what life's about. You think it's going to be all epic moments and big crowds, but almost all of life is the ordinary daily stuff and what we make of it. You don't want to wish it away or rush past it for the next big thing, because before you know it the months and years evaporate and if you're not careful you're left wondering what you did with the time.

Life's about what you do with the ordinary days.

God Bless Y'all

I cranked along a nameless back road in Arkansas. Enormous John Deere cotton pickers and mysteriously numbered roadside cotton bales provided fascinating activity as I passed through the first cotton harvest I'd seen. This country road seemed ideal for my ride, though I'd already learned the hard way to avoid the fluffy white tire-puncturing debris along the shoulders. Aside from an occasional truck hauling a huge cotton bale to the local gin, I encountered little traffic. It was a great morning to think and observe.

One aspect of our surroundings impacted Becky and me as we moved south. We both noticed an increasing contrast in the levels of poverty we encountered. On a warm morning beneath a glorious blue sky the disparity appeared especially stark.

The cotton fields seemed vast and virtually endless. I passed grand, prosperous-looking estates surrounded by rows of trees and manicured grounds. Clearly these were flourishing, thriving operations.

But along the same road I cranked past collections of horribly dilapidated shacks far beyond what I'd label as "shabby" or "rundown" homes. These weren't "neglected," at least on any scale I encounter in my relatively sheltered experience. These decaying buildings revealed a level of palpable hardship—juxtaposed with incredible abundance—for which I wasn't prepared.

I hadn't seen Becky for quite a while. Riding alone in such unfamiliar surroundings provided an interesting internal dilemma. There was always some small sense of loneliness and searching for the familiar trailer on the horizon. At the same time I loved the warm sunshine, the sweat, and the time to wonder about the stark differences within a single nation.

Finally I caught sight of the familiar white Subaru towing the Rich's Ride trailer. Becky drove past, made a U-turn, and eased to a stop on the shoulder in front of me. She and Monte climbed out and waited as I rolled behind the trailer.

By now this was a familiar routine—stock up on food, refill water bottle, scratch Monte's head, chat for a few minutes, and take time to rest and reconnect and figure out next steps. As we talked, we noticed a young man walking toward us.

He'd emerged from an especially rundown, decaying shed. Tarpaper over the windows, patches on a sort-of-a-roof, door flapping in the breeze—it was the sort of building I wouldn't have imagined someone lived in. This African-American man stopped about twenty feet away from us and drawled quietly, "I hear y'all are raisin' money."

He surprised us. We didn't expect anyone to come out of such an old building. We didn't expect to be approached on an apparently deserted stretch of country road. And we certainly didn't expect someone to know we were raising money.

Becky muttered, "Uh, yes, we are."

"Wait here." Then he retreated into the shack.

We made eye contact and silently acknowledged our fear. We believed we were in danger. I remember wishing Becky would jump into the car and get out of there. I was pretty sure we were about to be robbed, or worse. He didn't know we carried very little cash. I glanced around—no traffic, no one to help. We froze, uncertain, and waited because we weren't sure what else to do.

A few moments later the young man reappeared and walked slowly toward us. As he approached Becky he reached out and handed her a twenty-dollar bill.

"God bless y'all for what you're doing."

And he turned and disappeared back into the old shack.

We sat on the side of an isolated road, shook our heads, and tried to imagine what twenty dollars must have meant to someone who lived in that sort of home.

Later we surmised what must have transpired. We'd received quite a bit of television coverage in the area. Lots of drivers waved and honked as they passed during the day. The young man must have seen one of those spots and recognized our trailer as we parked in front of his house.

I judged him based on his appearance and the house in which he lived.

God saw his heart.

I've thought a lot about this incident. It would be awfully easy, in hindsight, to romanticize a God-inspired moment.

I'm ashamed of my reaction. As I said, I clearly judged a man based solely on outward appearance. His unexpected action shocked me. I didn't even say thank you. To be brutally honest, I was relieved when he walked away. It took me a moment to internalize what happened.

I wish I'd shaken his hand. I wish I'd asked about his family and taken time to learn a bit of his story. I wish I hadn't equated his identity with the place he lived. I wish I didn't have to wonder how the interaction would have happened differently if a well-dressed white man had approached us in front of one of those prosperous plantations.

I don't like that question. Maybe you don't like it either. Sorry about that. But some of the lessons are hard ones. Stepping out in faith sometimes takes you to uncomfortable places in the middle of nowhere.

Like I said before, let's not romanticize this episode. I probably should have gotten Becky to a safer place. Nothing wrong with being prudent, and there was legitimate reason for concern about her physical safety.

But my personal discomfort was all about being judgmental. You'd think a guy who lives in a wheelchair and gets indignant about being judged according to outward appearance would know better, but we're all subject to the same sins in different formats.

I saw a stereotype based on "poorly dressed black man who lives in a shack." God showed me a soft-spoken man with a humble, generous heart to remind me of what I miss when I see people through my biases rather than His eyes.

One of our pastors tells a story about a former gang member who found Jesus but still appeared to be living in the middle of nowhere. This man had a phrase tattooed on his knuckles: the second word was "you," and the first began with the letter "f"—and it wasn't "Philippians." I imagine this guy's appearance took many church folks to an uncomfortable spot in the middle of nowhere, a place they really didn't want to be.

Our church did a better job of demonstrating Jesus' heart than I did on an Arkansas country road. No point in regret, because God's about grace and forgiveness. Better to live with hope. I can only imagine what God did with those twenty bucks, how many times He multiplied it, and how many people He touched with an unexpected gift from a big heart.

When you follow a God-sized dream, some things go well and some don't. That's okay. You try to learn, and maybe you learn most from the mistakes. God's grace is pretty big, and it wouldn't be too far down the road before He'd provide a second chance.

Stepping out in faith sometimes takes you to uncomfortable places in the middle of nowhere. ▮

notes

20 shotgun house

Everyone has a story.

The first thing I learned in Greenville, Mississippi, was that I didn't say the town's name correctly. To my northern eyes the label on the map looked like "Green-ville." But the proper pronunciation is more like "Gren-vul" or, even better, "Gren-vul y'all."

The second thing I learned was the basis of the popular notion of "Southern hospitality." Greenville was one of many places where complete strangers welcomed us like old friends, even though we didn't speak the native language. Someone in Greenville heard about Rich's Ride; and before we even arrived we were all set up with complimentary hotel nights, media attention, and offers of free food. We were especially intrigued by an invitation to dine at the Shotgun House.

This establishment was everything you'd imagine in an authentic Southern barbeque joint. If you wanted fancy, try somewhere else. If you wanted plain old great food—ribs and brisket and fried chicken—in a setting likely unchanged in several decades, this was the right place. The toughest aspect of eating there was deciding among so many wonderful options.

The server took our order and delivered incredible food, with a reminder to save room for her homemade desserts. Aside from a couple of guys at the bar, we were the only customers, so she had time to chat. And just like so many other people we met, she wanted to tell us a story.

She spoke through tears of a friend, a young man injured as a child by a stray bullet. A drive-by shooting had left a sleeping toddler paralyzed below his neck. She talked about the boy's determination and perseverance against overwhelming odds. His attitude was a gift to her, and she wanted to thank us for what we were doing to encourage people like her young friend. Then she handed us a generous donation for Convoy of Hope. She thought a contribution in his honor would please him.

We asked if she'd be there tomorrow, if we could return with a copy of *Relentless Grace* for her and her friend. She said he'd be blessed by such a gift, but she was wrong.

Becky and I were the blessed ones.

Greenville was a great place for a rest day. We wandered a historic district filled with informational markers and signs commemorating significant locations and events. It was like a time machine, gazing at old churches and jazz clubs, imagining civil rights struggles and music legends on those same streets. We spent time with a newspaper reporter, a local who told us a lot about the town and its history. We did an interview for the evening television news. It was one of the most restful, relaxing days of the entire trip.

We returned to the Shotgun House, books in hand, grateful for the opportunity to try something else from the menu. The place was busy this evening, and Monte attracted the usual admiring smiles from the other diners. The local news appeared on the television above the bar and we recognized the reporter we met earlier. We wondered how our story would be presented.

As the newscaster introduced Rich's Ride, Monte's floppy-eared face filled the screen. The other folks in the room began to point and whisper as they recognized him and then Becky and me. When the feature ended, a man stood and approached our table. Monte greeted him, and he spoke to us after he'd provided a thorough ear-scratching. The Shotgun House provided another story.

He took out his wallet and handed Becky several bills. "Please take this in honor of my niece. She'd be amazed and pleased by what you're doing."

His niece was paralyzed in a car wreck as a high school senior. She recovered, completed high school, and received a bachelor's degree as a rehabilitation counselor. Now she worked as a rehab specialist and advocate for folks with disabilities. He explained how her amazing positive attitude had inspired him.

Once again we heard a thank-you for our journey and the inspiration we provided to people who were struggling. And again we knew we received by far the bigger blessing.

When I recall these incidents, when I relate them to others, I'm reminded of how many people face and overcome incredible adversity. Illness, injury, financial hardship, and relational pain aren't rare at all. Mostly it happens away from public view as people find ways to survive and then learn to flourish in apparently insurmountable situations. We heard so many tales like this, and I know they're only the tip of a very large iceberg. It's absolutely mind-boggling to realize what people do in the face of incredible adversity.

God's at work. In ordinary, everyday lives and events, He's present, bringing sense to senselessness. He's doing a new thing in powerful ways that so frequently go unnoticed. We were blessed to hear and experience so many of these stories.

This was the vision. It was never about the bike ride, not really. It was about sharing hope, offering one tangible bit of assurance that hope really does change what's possible. It was about opening doors and providing opportunities for others to convey stories of courage and resilience.

Hope doesn't guarantee happy endings. We didn't hear "happily ever after" at the Shotgun House. We imagine a world in which children aren't paralyzed by random bullets while they sleep and vibrant teens don't leave home in a car and return in a wheelchair. But in a broken and unjust world, pain and suffering are realities that don't disappear at the end of a magic rainbow.

I don't know why God permits such tragedy, but "why" doesn't really matter. He promises the pain is never pointless, and He promises to redeem and bring good from our struggles. That's the basis of hope that transforms the impossible into everyday one-degree miracles that change the world.

Everyone has a story. ∎

21 rolling fork

The world's filled with generosity, encouragement, and helpfulness. Turn off negative voices.

Finally, brothers and sisters, whatever is true, whatever is noble, whatever is right, whatever is pure, whatever is lovely, whatever is admirable—if anything is excellent or praiseworthy—think about such things. (Philippians 4:8)

I'm not especially fond of hospitals.

I once spent twenty-one consecutive weeks in a hospital. I appreciate the caring people who helped me through a terribly difficult season. I respect their gifts, knowledge, and skills, and their dedication to service. I'm grateful for folks who devote their lives to healing and to caring for those who can't be healed. I appreciate the network of professionals who collaborate to create our awesome health care system. But I'm not fond of hospitals.

Some unanticipated experiences on Rich's Ride inevitably involved less-than-optimal circumstances. On this sort of journey you can't possibly know what's around every corner, and unexpected episodes often end up making the best memories. However, if I'd known about the hospital before we started I probably would have declined.

Have I mentioned that I don't really care for hospitals?

When I cranked out of Greenville on Thursday morning I knew we were eventually bound for a weekend in Jackson. I left the hotel with a route and Becky's promise to figure out plans for the next night's destination. After winding my way a final time through streets drenched in Southern history, I headed south into cotton country. It was a cold morning, but thankfully the brisk breeze was a tailwind pushing me down the road.

On the outskirts of town I noticed a man running toward me. By now I'd learned this probably wasn't a threat, so I stopped and enjoyed his excitement about the television news story he watched as he prepared for work. He waved his coworkers across the busy street so he could introduce me as a celebrity. I smiled and shook hands and laughed at their excitement about meeting a crazy guy going for a bike ride.

A few miles later a truck pulled over. The driver jumped out and asked if we could take a picture together. He told me he'd been talking all morning about our project and handed me a twenty-dollar bill. As his truck disappeared a county sheriff's deputy approached. He turned on the flashing lights, made a U-turn, and pulled up behind me. As he stood and donned his smoky-bear hat, my mental stereotypes about Southern sheriffs kicked in. I imagined myself behind bars in a rural jail accused of breaking a local law prohibiting extreme stupidity. I hoped the good-old-boy justice of the peace would at least allow me to call Becky before sending me off to the chain gang. Note to self: I need to watch fewer movies.

Thankfully, I wasn't jail-bound. Instead, the deputy was on a mission from his boss to provide a police escort to the county line. I wanted to decline, but he said it would be "an honor." So I cranked along behind the flashing lights, feeling a bit silly but at the same time acknowledging that what seemed to me like a personal project was really something much bigger.

People respond to hope. In a culture so frequently portrayed as selfish and cynical, most folks want to believe in optimism, service, and gratitude. Most of all, people desperately, and often silently, want to believe their impossible dreams aren't impossible at all.

A small bit of faith in action is a powerful thing. I knew I didn't qualify as a poster boy for hope or confidence. But as I waved good-bye to my escort I reflected on the reality that anyone, even a bald crippled guy on a handcycle, has the power to encourage and inspire. Life isn't defined by ability or disability. You can empower others to follow God-sized dreams if you focus instead on possibility and availability.

Becky arrived just in time to see the deputy pulling away. Once she realized I hadn't been kicked out of town or arrested, she told me about our evening destination. We'd been invited to Rolling Fork.

Our new friend Lisa from the Greenville Visitors Bureau had contacted Becky and offered to help us with connections down the road. This sort of matter-of-fact generosity became common but never taken for granted during the trip. So Lisa made a phone call to her friend Meg Bickerstaff Cooper from Mississippi's Lower Delta Partnership, who immediately offered lodging and a speaking gig. It was too cold to sit for a long time, so Becky promised to stop me when she connected with Meg and learned about our plans in Rolling Fork. I resumed cranking as the trailer disappeared.

And you're probably still wondering about the hospital.

Grace and Bubba

This wasn't a day to enjoy a nice leisurely ride through the countryside. The biting north wind would have been miserable from any other direction, but today it pushed me along a nearly straight Southern road. I made great time, and as long as I pedaled I actually remained reasonably warm and comfortable. At about forty miles I was still going strong when I spotted the trailer in front of a roadside store. Apparently I was making even better time than I realized. As I rolled into the parking lot Becky and Monte ran from the building. "How did you get here so fast?" Even though my progress was wind-aided, it felt good to move faster than expected. That didn't happen very often.

Becky handed me some very hot soup. While I sipped and shivered, two men and a woman emerged from the building. As they walked toward us, Becky asked, "Did you see the sign?"

WELCOME. FARMERS GROCERY. GRACE, MISSISSIPPI.

Becky and Meg had arranged to meet at a crossroads named "Grace."

I sat on my bike and slurped rapidly cooling chicken noodle soup. As we braced against the stinging wind, Meg introduced her friend

Mark and her husband, Bubba. Whatever else happened, I knew our visit to Mississippi was complete because I got to meet—in person—a real, live "Bubba." He promised to tell some genuine redneck jokes once we reached a warmer spot.

It was too chilly to chat, so they shared only the essential details. Meg was still arranging accommodations in Rolling Fork (population approximately 2,500) and promised to connect us with the local newspaper. In the morning I was invited to speak to students at the high school. They assured us the entire town was excited about our visit and we'd have a great time.

I still had ten miles to pedal into Rolling Fork. Before I got too cold I arranged to meet Becky at the edge of town; said goodbye to Meg, Mark, and Bubba; and headed down the road.

About two miles out of town the road turned northeast, and a helpful tailwind became a nasty raw blast that stung my face and slowed my progress to a crawl. When I finally spotted Rolling Fork's water tower I was definitely ready to get off the bike and inside a nice warm hotel. As promised, Becky and Monte waited as I rolled over a bridge and into town. That's when I learned about the hospital.

When Meg promised a place to stay, she assumed a local motel would be available. She was dismayed to learn that Rolling Fork, like many small towns, had no handicapped-accessible rooms. It would have been easy to apologize and send us off to another town. But Southern hospitality doesn't surrender easily, and Meg wasn't about to break her promise. She called the administrator of the small community hospital, who offered to let us spend a night in one of his rooms.

In case you forgot, I'm not a fan of hospitals. I appreciated Meg's creativity, but I was definitely not excited about the prospect of a night as a voluntary hospital guest. As I followed Becky into the medical center parking lot I was busy inventing excuses for politely declining their kind offer. Then the welcoming committee showed up.

First, a guy who followed me into town waited in the parking lot so he could meet us, scratch Monte's ears, and offer a generous donation. As we talked, Sue and Jane emerged from the clinic, gushing about how wonderful it was that we came to Rolling Fork and how excited the entire town was to welcome us. They treated us like visiting royalty and didn't leave space for me to explain my reluctance. Before I could tell them why this wasn't a good idea they'd ushered us inside to the room they'd prepared and decorated, complete with goodie bags filled with snacks and souvenirs for Becky and me—and even a special one for Monte!

The newspaper reporter showed up to take pictures, and several staff members stopped by to welcome us and express appreciation for our visiting and speaking to the kids. We learned all about Rolling Fork's history as birthplace of the teddy bear. Google it—it's an interesting story. And before we knew what happened we were honored guests at Rolling Fork Community Hospital. Real hospitality just overwhelms you until all you can do is sit back and enjoy.

During the evening we received several donations and met an endless parade of wonderful people who brought us more food than we could consume in a week. They invited Monte for a walk, and he sniffed every single flower in their beautiful enclosed garden. Hospital staff wanted to give Becky a break and insisted on doing all of our laundry. We simply surrendered to their kindness and enjoyed one of the most relaxing evenings of the entire trip. I even slept well in a hospital bed.

Meg stopped by to confirm details of the school assembly. When I thanked her for the chance to meet an authentic "Bubba," she chuckled and said he fit the stereotype. She also told a cool story about the Grace store. Apparently there's an actual community called Grace. It's not indicated on most maps, so travelers often stop at the store to ask for directions. The proprietor enjoys being asked, "Can you help me find Grace?"

I think I'd like living on the road to Grace. Actually, I guess I do.

We did encounter one humorous language-related problem in Rolling Fork. I needed Internet access to update the blog, so Becky walked to the nurses' station to get the network password. She returned with a puzzled look.

"Did you get the password?"

"Yes," she laughed, "but it wasn't easy."

"Because ..."

"Well, I asked for the password. The man said it, and I tried to spell it to be sure I understood."

"Okay." This seemed like a bigger issue than it needed to be. I forgot we didn't speak the local language.

"So," she continued, "I started spelling what I heard. S-H-A-W-K ... . He interrupted, said I spelled it wrong, and repeated the word. So again I spelled S-H-A-W... . He interrupted again. We went back and forth several times, both of us getting a little frustrated. Finally I asked if he would write it for me. He handed me the paper. 'Shawkey,' he told me. 'It's the name of our county. Shawkey County, home of the teddy bear. The password is Shawkey.'"

"Shawkey" seemed like an odd name for a county, until Becky handed me the sticky note with the letters "S-H-A-R-K-E-Y."

Sharkey. Shawkey. Apparently we needed someone from "Gren-vul" to translate.

I still don't like hospitals, but those folks reminded me of the boundless compassion we encountered at every turn. Despite my efforts to escape to a familiar situation I could control, the kind people of Rolling Fork simply engulfed us with thoughtfulness and kindness.

The next morning we met with a great group of kids at a high school assembly. We all laughed as football and volleyball players tried to demonstrate how to ride the handcycle around the gym, and we shared interesting conversations with students and teachers. Pedaling out of Rolling Fork later that morning, I realized only about six days remained of Rich's Ride. After nearly two months, it was hard to even imagine life without a daily routine focused on five or six hours on my bike.

When the ride began nearly seven weeks earlier I resolved to focus on the present moment. I wanted to savor the process and enjoy each day rather than always looking to the destination. As the end of this incredible experience approached, I felt an occasional bit of sadness as I realized the ride would end much too soon. But on the road out of Rolling Fork I discovered a new perspective.

Dreams don't end.

One goal would soon be achieved. We'd enter New Orleans and conclude this particular project. But the story, the journey of hope, would continue. The final mile of this ride would represent the end of a single chapter in a much larger story, but the end of one chapter also signals the beginning of the next. The dream of sharing hope wasn't finished.

Just as the water's path doesn't truly begin in Lake Itasca, it doesn't end in New Orleans. The water falling into northern Minnesota collected into a stream that became the Mississippi River. The conclusion of the river isn't the end of the water because it flows into the Gulf of Mexico and begins another chapter in its journey.

Dreams are like that. Real dreams don't end. They grow and change; new chapters open as we reach previous goals. But the dream continues. It's left for us to decide whether we'll summon the courage to keep following.

The world's filled with generosity, encouragement, and helpfulness. Turn off negative voices. ▮

notes

22 i can do this

I'll bet Jesus never thinks, "You loved too much in that situation."

By the time we reached Jackson, Mississippi, we'd learned another lesson. The obvious stuff, the things we planned for and pointed toward, the events we tried to make important and central, usually weren't. We couldn't anticipate or script the most important encounters.

My cousin Rachel arranged for me to speak twice at her church. I was excited to meet and talk to the folks who worshiped at historic Galloway United Methodist Church in the heart of downtown Jackson. We were amazed to discover how accessible they'd made the old building while maintaining its authentic character. Sunday morning we gathered with a group from several adult Sunday school classes. Sunday evening we talked and laughed and had a great discussion with a high school youth group.

The morning group asked great questions and offered lots of encouragement and support. We met kind, gracious people who truly seemed to grasp the heart behind our project. This encounter was familiar and comfortable, precisely what I imagined when I pictured the ideal speaking gig.

Afterward a lady approached and asked if we'd consider staying in Jackson on Monday morning. She directed the church's homeless ministry, Grace Place, and invited me to speak to their guests. Of course I accepted her offer, and Becky began revising our Monday itinerary.

Early Monday morning brought a new and remarkably different audience. Sunday's group was polished and well dressed, pretty much a "typical" Sunday school environment. I was shocked that the same room in the same building could attract such radically different gatherings in the space of twenty-four hours. The previous day we were part of the family. This morning as I circulated and introduced myself I was clearly an outsider.

This was a tough-looking crowd, about what you'd expect from seventy-five guys who spent a cold, hungry, dangerous weekend on the streets. They showed up for a hot meal and a safe place to rest for a few hours. Becky, Monte, and I weren't what they expected, and they regarded an old guy and his weird bike suspiciously. Suddenly my presentation about a bike ride seemed woefully inadequate. I wasn't sure I knew how to speak words of comfort to men from a world I couldn't possibly understand.

Food was served, and the nice director lady introduced me. I probably exaggerated the skepticism I perceived in their faces. These men struggled to survive, and I felt like a stranger from the comfortable suburbs. A few guys dozed—frankly, I'd probably sleep, too, after shivering through a night of fear and uncertainty. But as I began I experienced a real sense of connection. It felt like they were searching for something they could embrace. I experienced a new understanding and an unexpected connection. My secure world might be irrelevant to them, but God's promises weren't. These guys desperately needed what I took for granted.

I felt myself grasping for the right words, and then the proper emotions, to help these guys connect with the dream behind Rich's Ride. There's a particular story I tell often when I speak. It felt like just the right message for this audience.

Leonard

Leonard was tired of my endless complaining. More than a year after my accident I still invested more energy in seeking sympathy than working to get better. He was sick of my lousy attitude.

Leonard was the latest in a series of physical therapists who tried to help me adjust to life with paralysis. We had an unspoken agreement: They worked hard while I complained and made excuses for not working at all. Leonard tolerated this waste of his time for a few sessions, but as he got to know me his patience diminished.

One day as I complained about the physical tasks I couldn't accomplish with my damaged body, he sat down in front of me with a blank sheet of paper. On one side he drew a circle around "10,000." He said, "I want you to imagine this circle represents all of the things you could do before your accident."

Then he turned the paper over and drew a similar circle with a pie-shaped wedge removed. He wrote "2,000" in the missing piece. "You just lost a lot of things, and you may never get many of them back. But now you need to make a decision.

"You can spend the rest of your life griping about the two thousand things you lost, or you can focus on the eight thousand that remain."

Concluding my Leonard narrative, I asked if anyone in my audience had ever lost something. Every person in the room—except the sleeping guys—raised a hand. I told them how I let my loss define me for a long time. In my mind, I was the guy who couldn't. Whatever it was, I couldn't do it.

"Has that happened to you?" Again, every hand went up.

"How would it be different if you focused on what you can do instead of what you can't?"

They got it. I could see the connection in their eyes.

I talked a lot about how it isn't easy, there's no magic solution, and it isn't going to change overnight. I tried to be transparent. I told the men I couldn't possibly understand their situation, didn't want to cover their pain with hollow platitudes. But I also told them I knew about hopelessness and I'd been to the place of giving up. I asked them to look past our obvious differences to see the shared struggle.

Then I asked if they thought my ride was easy. Heads slowly shook. It felt like they understood I wasn't just some guy who dropped in to toss around some empty God-words. And I ended with a challenge.

"If an old, bald, crippled guy can do this ride, what can you do?"

We finished. Guys began to move around, look at the bike. They hesitated, approached slowly, but eventually they said thank you or offered encouragement or asked a question. A tough-looking mid-twenties man pulled up a chair.

"I'm going to get out of this," he drawled, "but I'm not sure how." Between his thick Southern accent and street vocabulary I managed to make out perhaps two-thirds of the words of an incredible story.

He became a drug dealer in his teens, made a lot of money, and got involved in some very bad stuff. He skated on the edge of danger and somehow managed to escape the jail time and violent death that took most of his friends. He spoke of fatalism, of knowing when he quit school that he'd eventually end up incarcerated or buried. Except he didn't.

Somehow he found Jesus, or Jesus found him, or they found each other. He didn't have an explanation. He just knew one day that he didn't want "the life" any more. So, as hard as it was, he left everything he'd known. He quit.

And in quitting he encountered a brutal reality: no skills, no education, no family, no friends. "The life" had been his security, his support system, his family. Walking away meant leaving everything and stepping into nothing. He lived on the streets because he didn't know what else to do.

He didn't have it figured out. He knew he had none of what he needed to create a different kind of life, he acknowledged it was his fault, and he had little idea what to do about it. All he had as we talked was determination and faith that God wouldn't let him down.

He still faced a difficult path. I pray he held onto that determination and allowed God to show him the way out of his personal darkness.

While we talked I noticed a big man in a dirty green sweatshirt waiting calmly. As he walked directly toward me I could see tears streaming down his cheeks. He leaned over and gave me a huge burly hug.

With his head next to mine he whispered, "I can do this."

He stood, blinked away tears, and shook my hand. In a strong, clear voice he repeated, "I can do this."

Then he turned and strode out of the room.

I don't know what to do with stories like those. I found out later a bit of the backstory for these two men, and of course it wasn't as neat and clean as it seems when I relate highlights in a few paragraphs. Both faced huge, self-created obstacles. Both walked away confidently, but I know enough only to be certain neither experienced a quick, easy recovery.

Both knew Jesus and both took an important first step by acknowledging their mistakes. They had access to at least a minimal support system. But we all know it's not that easy.

I'll likely never know the outcomes of these two tales. But I know the proper seeds were scattered, and I trust the Gardener. That has to be enough.

I'll bet Jesus never thinks, "You loved too much in that situation." ▮

notes

23 canine philosophy

Life would be better if I could trust God as much as my dog trusts me.

The daily blog was one of the fun aspects of Rich's Ride. We shared stories and photos, offered real-time reflections, and maintained contact with the people who followed along. Not surprisingly, one of the most popular features of the blog was Monte's weekly contribution. I suppose I should be offended when my dog's writing attracts more attention than mine, but I'm accustomed to my role as part of Monte's entourage.

Monte filters a lot of the junk that gets in the way of communication and relationships. Since we're sharing the experience of this project, I thought you'd like to hear how it appeared from his perspective. And if this turns out to be your favorite chapter, I promise I won't be offended.

So ... enter Monte.

Hi. My name is Monte. I'm Rich's service dog, the good-looking one in all those photos, and I'm your official Thursday blogger for the next few weeks. Rich said something about being "too busy" with some big project and asked me to write some blog posts for him.

Since I'm going to be conversing with you, I'll let you in on a little secret, if you promise to keep it to yourself: Rich and Becky think I don't understand their conversations. They're wrong. I know exactly what they're saying, though most of it makes no sense.

Here's an example—I don't understand how Rich can be "too busy." I'm always busy. I'm busy eating, or playing, or sniffing, or getting my tummy rubbed. Lots of the time I'm busy sleeping. But whatever I'm doing, I'm totally into it. Wherever here is, that's where I am. I don't mess with past or future. I don't plan or worry. I just do stuff, and I'm always all-in.

So Rich says he's too busy, but I think he's choosing to do other things. That's okay, but he'd be better off to just say he's making different choices. "Too busy" sounds like he has no choice. Me? I'm always busy, but I never have too much to do.

Tomorrow when we go running, I'll just run until I'm done. I won't care how far or fast. If I'm tired, I'll stop. Rich will be watching a little screen with a bunch of numbers, measuring how far and how long. And he'll miss the interesting smells because he's thinking about what's next. I guess that's how you get too busy.

We're doing something called a "trip." I don't know what that means, but I have noticed lots of things are different. I don't have my nice cushy bed to sleep in. Eating's different, too. These days we get up at all sorts of times, and I don't get breakfast right away. And at night we seem to eat a lot later.

Rich takes me running in lots of strange new places. I'd love to explore all those new locations, but he keeps me leashed to the bike. It's okay. I still like running with him, though I'll never understand why we pass up interesting new stuff like it doesn't matter. It's the "too busy" thing, I guess. I'm never too busy to stop and explore.

Even though a lot of things are different, I know it'll be okay because I trust Becky and Rich. They always feed me. I don't know where the food comes from, but it's always there. So if it's in a new place or a little late I don't get worried. I know they'll feed me.

Same with sleeping—it's weird to always be in a new place, but as long as they're around I know it'll be okay. And when Rich takes me running, I just go wherever he goes. I don't even wonder if it's safe because I know he wouldn't take me someplace dangerous.

Becky and Rich talk a lot about something called God. I'm just a dog, so I can't understand something so big. But if I did, and I really believed in Him, I think I'd trust God the same way I trust Becky and Rich.

Trusting them makes life a lot easier for me. I can enjoy little things because I know they'll take care of big things. I wonder why they don't trust God like I trust them.

In the past few weeks I've heard Becky and Rich talk a lot about someplace called "home." They talk like home is a place and we're not there and they seem to miss it, and they wonder whether I miss it. But when they describe "home," they talk about the place where you're comfortable and safe and where you know people. "Home" sounds like where we are right now.

From what I can understand, the important thing about home is people. Even though we're in strange places, I'm with the people I care about the most, and there's lots of new people to meet and sniff and get tummy rubs from. It seems like I'm "home" as long as Becky and Rich are around.

So when they say they miss home and seem a little sad, I just do what I always do. I get close and try to get them to scratch my ears. I like it, and it always makes them smile. I think "home" isn't a place. When you're with the people you love and you're taking care of each other, I think you're at home.

One thing I don't get is the idea of "work" and "play." Rich and Becky always talk about them like they're different, but they seem the same to me.

When Rich drops something, I love picking it up and giving it back to him. It's fun, and it makes me feel good. They call that work. When he throws a tennis ball, I love chasing it and bringing it back. They call that play.

I don't see the difference.

Humans seem to think work shouldn't be fun. When I pick up something for Rich I'm not supposed to pounce on it or shake it or anything. I'm supposed to just pick it up and quietly put it in his lap. B-O-R-I-N-G! Why not add some laughs? If the job still gets done, what's wrong with turning it into a game?

I guess it's "work" if it's something they want and "play" if it's something they think I want. I think we'd all be better if we did stuff we liked and didn't worry about whether it's work or play.

Rich is doing this "project" I don't really understand, but I think it must be a pretty good thing. He's working really hard, he's always tired, and I think he's having a lot of fun. I can't tell if it's work or play. I think that's how it should be.

Last time I told you we're involved in something called a "project." I'm trying to understand how projects are different from jobs.

Rich and I don't go to school every day anymore because he retired from his "job" as a teacher. I miss being with kids, and I think Rich does, too. I've heard him say he misses kids but doesn't miss the job.

Apparently a job makes you show up and do what someone else tells you to do, even if it doesn't make any sense. As long as you have a job you get money, which seems kinda like getting treats.

I'm glad I don't have a job. I love getting treats and figuring out what I'm supposed to do for them, but I wouldn't like having to do unpleasant tasks because I'm afraid I'd starve.

I told you how work and play are the same to me. It seems like that's what happens with a project. You think up something big and important, and then you work hard to do it. Only the work is really fun. I like that idea—or I'd like it if dogs could have ideas.

Projects always seem to involve other people. Whenever Becky or Rich start a project, they get a team together. That makes sense. When I'm hungry and I can't get my food out of the container, Rich helps me. And sometimes Rich drops something and can't reach it, so I help him. We're a team. That's how projects appear to work. Everybody gets to do what they're good at to help each other.

Jobs seem like you mostly do them by yourself. I wouldn't be good at a job, because when I'm by myself I mostly just sleep. I wonder if people feel like that.

Projects are cool because something big happens. I don't really understand, because dogs don't think about big stuff. I envy people—they can dream and follow their dreams. I'd like to be able to do that, I think. I mostly just chase tennis balls and Frisbees.

One thing I don't get is that people can follow their dreams, but most of them don't seem to do it much. Lots of them just settle for jobs and act like working on dreams is silly or irresponsible. Or they spend lots of time figuring out ways to avoid doing anything at all.

I love doing stuff, and I think I'd like dreaming up important goals and working on them. I'm just a dog, so I can't do that. But if I could, I hope I wouldn't waste such an important ability.

Rich and Becky both did projects as part of their jobs (when they had jobs) and it seemed like it's when they were happiest. They do projects all the time at home and we have fun. And we're doing this big project now, which they seem to think is lots of fun even though they're really tired every night.

So I think it must not be the work that wears people down. It must be jobs. I'm glad I get to work without having a job.

I'm trying to figure out my role in what's happening.

You all know we're doing this thing called Rich's Ride. For me it's not a big deal, because I just do what I always do. Rich and Becky tell everyone we're a team, which I think means we each do what we're good at. But I've been wondering how I contribute to the team.

I might have an idea—or as close to an idea as a dog can have.

The other night we went to this restaurant where they throw rolls at you. This is a dog's dream, because there were plenty of crumbs on the floor.

Anyway, this nice lady walked over and started talking to Becky, admiring how beautiful I am. This happens just about everywhere we go. She scratched my ears and rubbed my backside, and I thought she was great.

But then the lady took out something she called a "checkbook," wrote something, and tore out a paper and handed it to Becky. I don't know anything about checks, but Becky was delighted and I liked that. She thanked the nice lady and told her the gift would help feed hungry children. I have no idea how that works, but I'm in favor of anything related to eating. And I love stuff that makes Becky or Rich happy.

This has happened many times. Someone walks up to us and starts talking about how wonderful I am, and Becky uses the opportunity to tell them about what our team is doing. They get all excited, and while they scratch my head they hand Becky one of those checks or some money. Then Becky gets all happy and thanks them and tells them they're helping hungry children.

I don't think this would happen if I wasn't here, so I guess I really am part of the team. I'm happy to contribute, especially since I'm just being my adorable self.

Teams and projects must be good things. We get to do fun stuff that seems to make just about everyone feel good. What's better than doing things you enjoy with people you like and making everyone happy?

I wonder why we don't do this all the time.

We're in another new place called the South. I don't know what that means—it's just another place with unique smells to check out. But I have noticed something I don't like very much: People keep asking Becky and Rich if I bite.

It started a few days ago. Strangers began to shy away like I'm dangerous or scary or something. And even people who seem to like me are slow to approach, asking Becky or Rich if I bite. What a weird question. Of course I don't bite! Why would anyone even ask such a thing? In my whole life I don't think anyone's ever asked if I bite.

Oh, I do bark once in a while, but it's just my way of saying hello and playing. A dog's gotta let folks know who's in charge, right? But I've never bitten anyone. Why would someone assume I bite before they've even met me? Frankly, it kinda hurts my feelings.

I guess dogs must be different here. I'm glad I don't live in a place where people are afraid of me. I think it must be awful to have fear as a first reaction to something new.

I think people here must be afraid a lot. Maybe this is a scary place. Maybe there's a reason to be scared, something I don't understand because I'm just a dog. I always just trust people. It feels yucky to be with people who are suspicious and afraid.

They hide it most of the time, but if they're afraid of me they must fear other stuff.

I think that's sad.

Becky and Rich talk a lot about love. It confuses me.

They tell each other, "I love you," and they both tell me they love me. Rich says he loves riding his bike. Becky loves fancy coffee. And they tell people I love to chase tennis balls.

So let me see if I understand—Rich feels the same way about his wife, his dog, and his bike. Am I the only one who has a hard time figuring out what "love" means? I think when they use the word love so much, it almost doesn't mean anything.

There's something else I hear a lot. People keep saying I show them what love is really about. That's nuts—I'm a dog. But since they seem to think I know about love, I figured I'd list some of the things that make them think I know about love.

***I don't judge people**. When someone new appears, I check them out. If they're nice, I hang around. And I give them lots of chances to be nice, because new people mean more chances to get petted and scratched. I don't care what they wear or what they look like. I can't figure out why those things would matter.*

It takes time for some people to like me. That's okay—I've got lots of time, and if someone ends up being my friend it's worth it. Some humans decide whether they'll accept someone before they get to know them, sometimes before they even meet. How can you decide until you get to know them?

I forgive. *Rich and Becky do stuff I don't like. Sometimes they leave me at home by myself, or they feed me late. Rich takes off on his bike without me. But nobody's perfect, so what's the point in getting angry? So as soon as I can, I wag my tail and show them it's okay. And they scratch my ears and seem relieved that I'm not upset.*

I serve. *Now, let's be clear—I'm a dog. I do stuff for treats. But isn't it cool to get what makes me happy by doing stuff that helps people? I like doing stuff for Rich, even when he forgets to give me a biscuit. You'd think people who are much smarter than me could figure out that it feels good to do something for someone else.*

Love seems like kind of a simple idea, but maybe I'm missing something. After all, I am only a dog.

Enter Rich again.

Looking back through Monte's reflections, I think I understand why he was the star blogger. He sees through simple eyes and observes what really matters. He focuses on relationships, trust, love, and tummy rubs. At some level, we all know we'd be better off if we did the same. We all know life would make more sense if we simplified and concentrated on core issues. We know that's exactly what Jesus tells us.

Life would be better if I could trust God as much as my dog trusts me. ▮

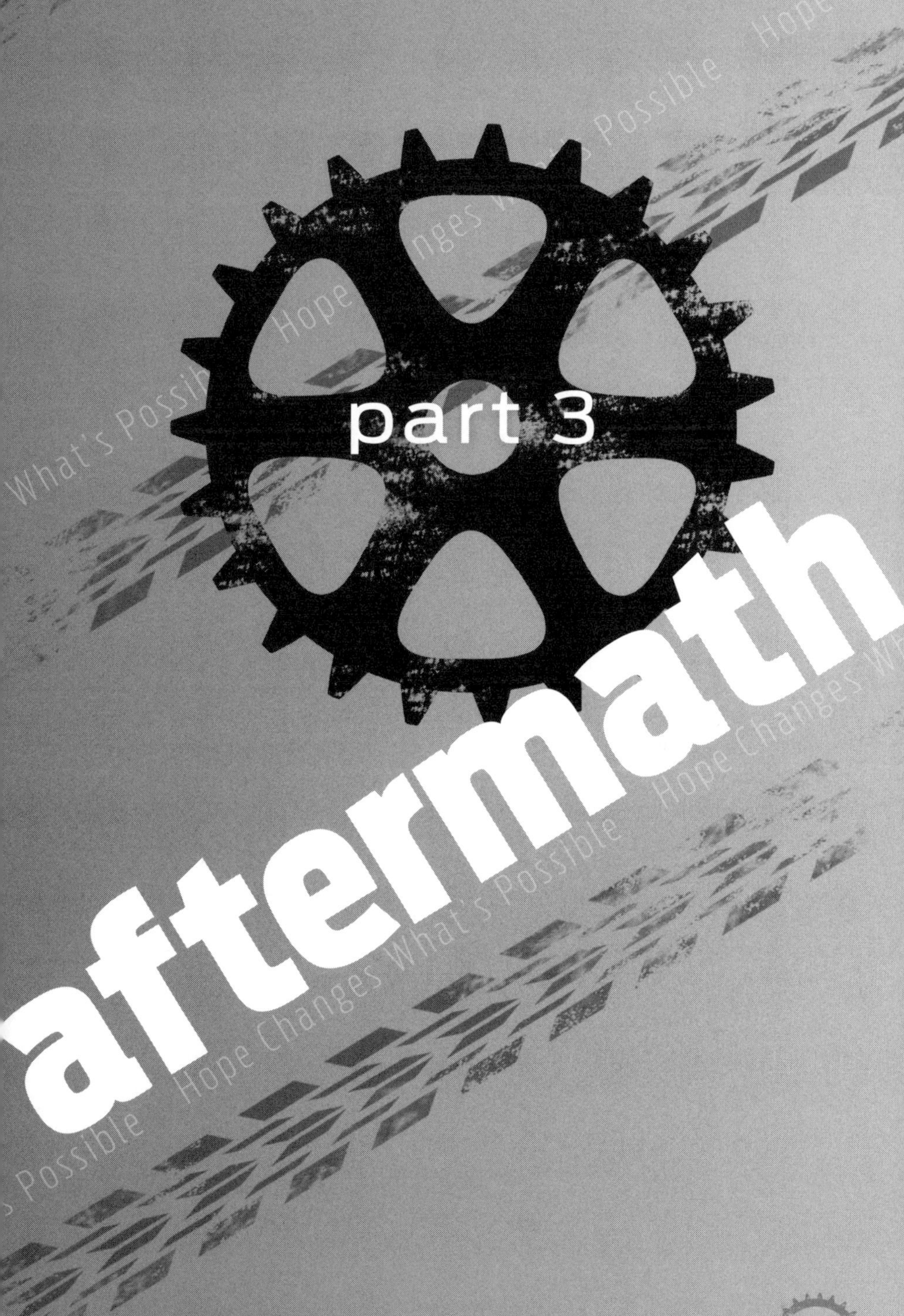

part 3

aftermath

24 success!

The numbers we use as "measurables" rarely reflect the true purpose of what we're doing.

How do you define success?

We asked that question in the planning stages, but I'm not sure we formulated a coherent answer. We were quite honestly into something much bigger than we could even imagine, and we just didn't know what might happen. We had hopes and dreams, but we avoided stating a clear definition of success because we couldn't think big enough.

Our vision of what was possible grew as the ride progressed. As we approached the finish line I felt we'd been successful in just about every aspect of the project, but I also wondered exactly what "success" meant. So many people invested time, talent, and treasure to support my efforts. It's natural to wonder about their ROI (Return On Investment). Did we accomplish anything? Did those supporters get their money's worth?

I taught mathematics to teenagers for thirty-five years. Like most good teachers, I learned much more from my students than they learned from me. When I began teaching I thought it was about knowing all the right answers. I found that teaching, like life, is less about knowing the right answers and more about asking the right questions.

"Success" simply means accomplishing an aim or purpose. Nobody establishes an important target and then intentionally misses it, so every person or organization seeks success. Success involves hitting the target.

The real question, the one that matters, is "What's the target?" What are you trying to accomplish? What's the true purpose or motivation behind your efforts?

On the last day of the ride we reflected on several numbers:

- *1,500 miles*
- *8 weeks*
- *9 states*
- *37 miles averaged per day*
- *51 miles on the longest day*
- *9 mph average speed*
- *13 mph best average speed for a single day*
- *26 speaking events*
- *More than 4,000 people reached in speaking venues*
- *Nearly $60,000 raised for hungry children*
- *Approximately 1,200 children fed for an entire year*
- *More than $25,000 donated in sponsorship for the ride*

Those numbers matter. In business terms they're the measurables, the subject of charts and graphs and calculations. They're important indicators of a track record if I seek funding for future rides. This project required substantial support to pay for transportation, food, lodging, and equipment. The only place these realities can be ignored is called Fantasyland.

The numbers are important, but they don't measure what was important about Rich's Ride. We might have increased every number and still been unsuccessful, and the numbers might have been significantly worse on a ride that was a smashing success. It's an important lesson: The numbers we use as "measurables" rarely reflect the true purpose of what we're doing.

On the final day of riding we completed the fifteen-hundred-mile goal in a small town on the outskirts of New Orleans. Dick DeCook flew from Colorado to join us for the final miles. Dick, Becky, and I celebrated a bit, exchanged high-fives, and stood around wondering what should happen next. We snapped pictures, stowed the equipment for a final time, and prepared to drive the final few miles into the city.

Despite the day's epic accomplishment, a few mundane daily necessities still required attention. We stopped at a small community hospital so I could use the accessible restroom. While Becky waited in the lobby, a man and two women called her over and asked her to tell them about "Hope on Wheels." Apparently they'd seen the trailer as we rolled into the parking lot.

So Becky told the story, and I appeared in time for them to express admiration and astonishment. We chatted, mostly small talk, for a few moments. Then Becky's phone rang and she stepped outside to finalize arrangements for a weekend speaking event. This trio looked exhausted, and I asked what was happening.

This man and his two sisters had arrived eighteen days earlier when "Momma" suffered a stroke. After eighty-five strong, healthy years as family matriarch, Momma lay incapacitated and weak. Her children wept as they verbalized their emerging realization—Momma might not recover.

They asked me to tell them about hope.

Platitudes and easy answers just don't work in that sort of situation. We talked about love and faith in the midst of this pain, and the big guy whispered, "What can we believe when the docs say Momma probably won't get better? Where can we find hope in that?"

"I don't know what's going to happen, but we know this—God's taking care of her, right?"

He smiled. "You're right, and she knows that. She knows Jesus is with her."

He and his sisters were laughing through tears. "Remember her singing about the 'glory of heaven' while she washed dishes?"

Then things suddenly got quiet again. They remembered where they were.

The man said, "So that's hope?"

"Maybe that's part of it—knowing God keeps His promises, knowing He'll care for her no matter what. And knowing He'll care for you folks as well."

I showed them the back of my bike jersey. They read it quietly: HOPE changes what's possible.

The sisters shook my hand and walked outside. The big guy hugged me; and as he leaned close, I whispered, "Momma's gonna be okay."

"I know."

That's hope.

The numbers we use as "measurables" rarely reflect the true purpose of what we're doing.

I don't know how to measure that moment. I can't chart it or calculate its value. I don't know how to figure it into our sponsors' ROI. But such interactions do reflect the central purpose of Rich's Ride. It was a divine appointment, and those folks were some of the unnamed people for whom we prayed before the ride began. We asked God to guide us to those who needed a message of hope and encouragement. We prayed for open hearts, for a willingness to be flexible. We asked for the right words and for the presence of His Spirit when words weren't sufficient.

We prayed our request nine weeks earlier. On this final day of the ride we experienced God's faithful answer yet again. We thought the day was all about celebrating our big accomplishment. I'm glad God kept our hearts open and sensitive to opportunities.

An Able-Bodied World

Two days later we met in New Orleans with a group called Handicapped Encounter Christ (HEC) including people with a variety of disabilities and the "able-bodied" folks who supported their ministry. A small group, perhaps twenty-five people, sat on a patio and shared a great discussion about disability ministries.

I began as I often do with a small audience, by asking what they wanted me to talk about. After a short pause, Kristin began the discussion with a startling statement posed as a question. I'm frankly still a bit flustered as I reread her words.

"You're doing this amazing project that inspires everyone, especially people like us. Can you tell us how you're able to function so well in an able-bodied world?"

Before reading further I invite you to ponder those words for a moment. What stands out for you?

I think I lightened the mood, and stalled for time, by suggesting my friends might offer a different view of her assumption that I "function well." Everyone chuckled while I searched for a response to Kristin's challenging question. I think I understood her intent, but the words revealed something deeper and more significant.

"People like us."

"An able-bodied world."

Am I part of "us"? If so, who's "them"? Do I truly live in "an able-bodied world"? An able-bodied world might tolerate me, even make allowances for me, but I'm at best a resident alien. A guy who's paralyzed below his chest cannot claim full citizenship in an able-bodied world.

Kristin's question assumed God created the world for people who meet some arbitrary physical standards. I guess those of us who fall short ought to stay out of the way and feel grateful we're allowed to hang out on the edges.

I'm not blind to reality. I clearly face a unique set of physical challenges. There's no point in pretending. But words have incredible power to shape our attitudes. Description becomes perception, and perception becomes reality. An "able-bodied world" marginalizes me and many of the folks in my audience.

I see it differently. As a wheelchair user, I encounter many labels.

Handicapped, disabled, physically challenged—what should others call me? Personally, I prefer "Rich."

I'm not a wheelchair. My friend with MS isn't a disease. My former student with impaired sight isn't a white cane. We're all people with strengths and weaknesses, just like every other person. Why must we segregate individuals by labeling them as "special," pretending others are "normal"? Does the label imply most folks aren't special, or they don't have needs, or their needs aren't special?

What's "normal?" When my car operates normally, it's performing as the designer intended. Which of us operates as God intended when He designed us? Apparently, the only normal person who ever lived was Jesus; the rest of us are flawed, broken, not operating according to design specifications.

My physical impairment is visible, and I deal with it daily. But what about my spiritual impairments—do I confront them as readily? Am I guilty of labeling others with "spiritual special needs" as though I'm somehow in a better category of sinner? Do I pretend that my flaws are "normal"?

God doesn't see me as a category, and He didn't create an able-bodied world. Each of us is a unique, precious individual in His eyes. Each of us falls short of the glory for which He designed us, and each of us is so special that He sent His Son to restore us to full operating capacity.

Evening faded, shadows lengthened, and discussion waned. But they were intensely curious about the ride's logistics and equipment, and the real fun happened when we went across the street to show off the bike.

One young lady named Phong wanted to try it. Phong might be 4 feet 8 inches tall, so we had some good-natured fun getting her situated on a bike configured for my 6-foot-1-inch frame. But she slipped easily from her smaller chair onto the bike seat and we figured out some accommodations. Soon she was zipping around the parking lot, dodging cars, with a huge smile on her face.

"I gotta get one of these!"

While I called out encouragement, we all laughed and shared in her unbridled, passionate joy. Several others worried a careless driver might interrupt her fun, but I blinked away tears. Phong's grin displayed the same sense of wind-in-the-face freedom I experienced on my initial two-block cruise more than ten years earlier. The handcycle broke an invisible barrier for both of us. Maybe you can't comprehend the value of that sort of liberty unless you've lost it. Weaving past a few inattentive drivers is a small risk when the reward is freedom.

Maybe, in the face of an able-bodied world, Phong's smile defines success.

The numbers we use as "measurables" rarely reflect the true purpose of what we're doing. ▮

notes

25 next?

The dream's invitation continues.
We decide only whether we'll keep following.

A dream is a story waiting to be written.

Dreams, at least the kind of dreams I've tried to describe, are inspired. The word "inspired" implies breathing, taking in something life-giving or life-sustaining. I believe God places in your heart a desire to serve in your own unique capacity, to imagine something beyond yourself and your own comfort. You're wired to answer that life-giving call.

Inspiration invites, opening a door and providing a glimpse into a remarkable future. It stands in the door and calls us to step into an adventure, an unknown new world of imagination, challenge, and opportunity.

Inspiration illuminates, shining its light on a path of possibility and faith. Inspiration provides a compass but rarely a map. It points the way and promises to reveal the next step when we need to know it.

Inspiration encourages—it supplies courage. It offers the character-developing opportunity to face fear and move forward with confident expectation.

Inspiration leads. It goes first and invites you to come along on an adventure. Motivation pushes, usually from behind, often with external rewards like money, attention, approval, or fear. I don't think dreams rely much on motivation.

Dreams may ultimately generate those sorts of rewards, but they're not the driving force. We received a fair amount of attention and approval, and raised a sizable chunk of money, but those were pleasant side effects. External motivations cloud the joy of following a dream. They color judgment, complicate decision-making, and drive us in directions other than the dream's intended path. Maybe it works out sometimes, but I think it's a tough way to pursue a dream.

Should I Follow?

A dream is the God-inspired desire to share your unique gifts and passions to serve others and change the world.

Are you wondering about following your own dream?

I hope you are. I hope you're listening to a prompting to share and serve and make a difference. I hope you're standing at the edge, wondering if this is the moment to jump, feeling the thrill and the fear, hearing the call and wondering how to answer. I hope you're weighing the risks of yes against the potential regrets of no.

The story of Rich's Ride frequently prompts others to tell me about their dreams. I'm inspired by so many exciting notions of hope and possibility, and I'm reminded that dreams invoke both enthusiasm and anxiety. These heart-stirring stories often conclude with a question: Do you think I should do it?

God wants us to dream bigger than we can imagine and trust Him for what's beyond our own capabilities. He inspires outrageous visions even in those who don't believe in Him. I encourage everyone to listen and respond to God's promptings, but I don't advocate impulsive commitments. I haven't developed a step-by-step process for evaluating a dream's validity, and I hesitate to advise someone else to jump into pursuit of a particular vision.

I fussed with my notion of a cross-country bike ride for more than a decade, and I still don't fully understand how it developed. I can explain, in retrospect, some of the circumstances that converged to make 2011 the right time, but I can't claim I perceived what was happening as it occurred. During all those years I imagined it, wished about it, and felt certain it didn't make sense ... and then it did. I believe my ultimate sense of certainty came from God.

A God-inspired desire doesn't live in a nice little box with crisp, clear boundaries. Every attempt to confine a dream changes it. If you hack away enough at the perplexing edges, you transform the dream into a human-created plan that isn't a dream at all. God-inspired desires aren't comfortable and safe and predictable. Dreams show up like Jesus at the seashore. "Come, follow me," Jesus said, "and I will send you out to fish for people" (Mark 1:17). You decide to follow even when you don't understand exactly what it all means.

A dream offers a choice that shouldn't be taken lightly. Perhaps it's wise to hang out with it awhile before making a commitment. Pray about it and listen to the response. Talk to those you trust. Examine your heart and your motives, because committing to a dream has consequences. You can't anticipate most of them, but it's good to count the obvious costs.

Following a dream isn't blindly jumping off a cliff. As responsible stewards we seek to care for what God's entrusted to us and invest our gifts wisely and intentionally. Stepping out in faith doesn't imply being reckless or foolish.

But responsible stewardship isn't risk-free. Jesus reprimanded a fearful servant who hid what was entrusted to him (Matthew 25:14–30). Our gifts and passions are meant to be used, to empower us for service. Responsible dream-following requires wisdom and careful discernment to distinguish justified from irrational risk.

You'll never make a difference if you insist on eliminating every potential hazard. If you seek logical reasons to avoid a dream, you'll find more than you imagined. There are plenty of reasons to say no, so the final choice to follow a dream can't be made with a balance sheet. God-inspired desires often make no objective sense to others, or even to you. In the end the choice to follow or not is more heart song than reasoned analysis.

My closest friends would tell you the prospect of Rich's Ride frightened them. They thought I was ignoring reality and assuming unnecessary risks. I rejected perfectly sensible suggestions that just didn't feel right. Hindsight shows I chose correctly at times and unwisely at others. But I chose based on a place in my heart.

If you're wondering about following a dream, perhaps the real question is *What's stopping you?* If the dream seems like a God-inspired desire, "what's stopping you" is most likely fear. Perhaps the dream is God's invitation to choose courage, confront the fear, and respond rather than react.

When the disciples saw Jesus walking on the water, they were afraid. Jesus said, "Take courage! It is I. Don't be afraid" (Matthew 14:27).

"Take courage." Jesus didn't tell us to deny fear, because where there's no fear there's no need for courage. He offers a better way, an opportunity to respond courageously despite our fear because He's always with us.

Should you follow a particular dream? No one else can answer that question.

A dream is an elusive thing.

Prepare and Train

I talked earlier about the difference between *doing* and *having done*. I think you have to *follow* the dream. A dream is a story waiting to be written; *follow* inspires you to write the story. *Follow* engages and creates a shared journey. I suspect you'll struggle if you seek the experience of *having followed*.

Dreaming is great, but at some point you have to start. The only way to write a great story is to begin writing. If you're wondering how to start following, here's an idea from Old Chain of Rocks Bridge: Stop planning. Start preparing.

You can't really plan a dream, because adventures don't come with pre-scripted itineraries. Plans create the illusion of progress, but mostly they're a good way of putting off the real work. You'll need some plans eventually, but you begin following by preparing.

A dream is the God-inspired desire to share your unique gifts and passions to serve others and change the world.

rich's ride *By Rich Dixon*

I prepared for Rich's Ride for more than ten years. Mostly I didn't know I was preparing or understand what I was preparing for, but that's okay. The dream's God-inspired, not me-inspired. Dreams have to be followed on God's timeline.

Part of preparing involves discovering and developing your unique gifts and passions, because dreams invite you to do what you love. During those years I discovered my love for handcycling. I learned that I enjoyed writing, and I wrote and published *Relentless Grace*. I established and developed a community around my blog. My personal life stabilized as I came to terms with my injury and reconnected with lost love. I got to know Jesus better, learned a little more about how to hear God's voice, and discovered a faith community to circle me with encouragement and support.

I can't imagine Rich's Ride without this foundation I could never have envisioned or constructed on my own. Some of the preparing was intentional, but a lot was simply trusting God and doing what appeared before me. The dream's God-inspired, not me-inspired.

So if you're not sure about following your dream, perhaps you can start preparing by discovering and developing your gifts and passions and doing what's in front of you.

Training is another important part of following. If you're wondering about how to begin, consider this notion: *Stop trying. Start training.*

You can't really *try* to follow a dream. You either follow or you don't. If you're frustrated with trying so hard and not getting results, here's a tough question: Have you done the required training?

If you try as hard as possible to run a marathon next weekend, you'll most likely fail. But you can *train* for a marathon. If you train well, you'll be much better prepared for the desired result. Important outcomes are built on habits, small improvements, and simple daily acts that make up the training. Small things, done faithfully and consistently, add up to something big.

Dreamers train with joy because training's part of following. Training involves doing what you love because you're immersed in your gifts and passions. If you hate the training, if you endure it only to get somewhere else, perhaps you're not truly following.

You can't train all at once. It takes a long time and sometimes you can't see any progress. Training requires faith. You have to believe that all of those hours will add up to something important, even when you can't see it. It takes perseverance and determination. Trying hard might not get you much. But if you stop trying and start training, you change the one thing you need most. When you train you change yourself.

Earlier I talked about two questions integral to the project's DNA. I've tried to answer Why? Now it's time to tackle What's next?

At nearly every gathering, beginning at the initial meeting on Elk River Day, folks asked about future plans. Listeners innately sensed something bigger than an eight-week bike ride.

"Let's see how this ride goes," I'd joke, but the question's continued presence conveyed an important message. Perhaps fifteen hundred miles represented nothing more than a good start on the path marked out by our God-sized dream. This reality struck me on the road from Rolling Fork when I understood the distinction between dream and goal and concluded, "Dreams don't end."

I don't know if all dreams continue indefinitely. Perhaps some arrive with built-in expiration dates. I'll leave that to the dreamers and the God who inspires them.

I do know this journey didn't conclude in New Orleans. Our dream of sharing hope isn't finished. One goal achieved doesn't fulfill my God-inspired desire to travel together on this journey of hope.

I'm tempted by the trap of needing to know the entire path ahead, because old habits die hard. This fifteen-hundred-mile expedition taught me the need to trust that I'll see where to go when I get there. It's uncomfortable, but it's the nature of dream-following.

I trust He'll guide me to the right doors and open them at the proper times. Right now, this book is my answer to "what's next." So

I write and edit, not because I seek to publish a book but because it's the next step in following. It's what I can do right now, right here, with what God's given.

Other bike rides await. We're exploring options and opportunities. In my head I wonder if I can commit to something outrageous like accumulating ten thousand miles of adventures similar to our Mississippi River journey. I suppose it depends on, among other things, how long an old body holds out.

We'll update developments and ideas on the Rich's Ride website (www.richsride.org). I hope you'll check out the site and recommend it to others. I hope you'll subscribe and follow along and meet us if our journey brings us near your corner of the world.

However, I believe the ubiquitous presence of "What's next?" demonstrated something deeper than simple curiosity about our personal plans. People connected with this project because hope resonates in every heart. Others see an old, bald, crippled guy doing something this outrageous and wonder about their own capabilities. I believe they feel a stirring somewhere inside, maybe in a place they've tried to ignore because it seemed impractical or impossible. I believe Rich's Ride challenges our definition of impossible, because hope changes what's possible.

Maybe "what's next" really seeks to know if God-sized dreams can be sustained beyond a one-time event. Maybe when someone understands that this dream continues she can face her true question: "How can I find the courage to follow my own dream?"

The invitation beckons. The dream continues. The opportunity to do something remarkable and write an amazing story remains. The God-inspired desire to serve and change some small corner of the world still calls. I hope sharing this journey spurs you to listen and find your own dream.

So I'll conclude with a challenge. If you're pondering your own God-sized dream I'll leave you with a couple of tough questions.

"If an old, bald, crippled guy can crank a handcycle fifteen hundred miles, what can you do?"

"What's next?"

The dream's invitation continues.
We decide only whether we'll keep following. ▮

acknowledgments

Find excuses to celebrate.

Rich's Ride Sponsors

OtterBox Corporation and OtterCares Foundation

Timberline Church

Acorn Creative Studio

First National Bank

Spradley Barr Motors

The Body Fitness Center

Jax Outdoor Gear

GoPro Cameras

Top End Handcycles

Yancey Food Services

Poudre Valley Health System

Everitt Companies

Dellenbach Motors

Rocky Mountain Recumbents

Becky and I wish to thank everyone who made Rich's Ride possible. We appreciate the financial support of the companies and organizations listed above. Their generosity characterizes the incredible spirit of our community. We also thank our core advisory group—Pastor Dick Foth, Pastor Mark Orphan, Dick DeCook, and Dave Goldfain—for their guidance and wisdom.

We especially wish to thank Kurt and Nancy Richardson, owners of OtterBox Corporation of Fort Collins and benefactors of OtterCares Foundation. Kurt and Nancy caught the vision of Rich's Ride and led the way as our initial sponsors. Their generosity and incredible corporate citizenship are a shining example of a company dedicated to doing well and doing good.

We also thank our friends Becky and Rock Adams of The Body Fitness Center in Fort Collins for arranging and hosting a wonderful send-off party. Their generosity allowed us to physically experience a part of the circle surrounding this project.

Finally, we're honored and humbled by the boundless support of our faith community at Timberline Church. They adopted a most unlikely missions project and supported us with love and prayer.

We didn't go on Rich's Ride—we were sent.

Hosts and Riding Companions

Mark & Paulette Dixon

Steve Moore

Kelley McGowan

Michael White

Larry Hackett

Greg Schibbelhut

Kevin & Lynn Schwendinger

Lesley Dakin

Glenn & Judy Bruckhart

Bruce & Sandy Payne

Dale Crall

Dudley & Melissa Boyd

Vic Evans

Rich & Beth McClure

Meg Bickerstaff Cooper (& Bubba)

Rachel & Moise Kabukala

Kristin Cipriani

David Grant

Kirk Noonan

Hal Donaldson

Books don't happen in isolation. One guy gets to claim authorship, but many people contributed time, talent, and vision to create these pages. Thanks to Mary McNeil for her gifted editing eye and to everyone at Simple Plan Media for their patience and dedication in producing a high-quality book. Any remaining errors or omissions are mine.

This book is the story of a dream, and it couldn't have happened without the people who shared their stories along the way. We appreciate their honesty, generosity, and vulnerability. We pray that each person continues to follow the vision cast by their own dream.

Find excuses to celebrate.
Fort Collins, Colorado
September 2012

Please continue to follow Rich's Ride:

www.richdixon.net

www.richsride.org